FROM THE

LIBRARY OF

JOHN VOOYS 1987

LIVING
BY
THE GOSPEL

Living by the Gospel

Christian Roots of
Confidence and Purpose

◆

Klaus
Bockmuehl

HELMERS & HOWARD

Colorado Springs
Colorado 80933

Published by Helmers & Howard, Publishers, Inc., P.O. Box 7407, Colorado Springs, CO 80933.

Library of Congress Cataloging-in-Publication Data

Bockmuehl, Klaus, 1931—
  Living by the Gospel.

  1. Christian life—1960-   . I. Title.
BV4501.2.B595   1986   248.4   86-27124
ISBN: 0-939443-01-5

Printed in the United States of America

CONTENTS

FOREWORD

This I read years ago: "It's a very odd thing/ Just as odd as can be/ That whatever Miss T. eats/ Turns into Miss T." Odd? Yes, but true! So we should be careful what we eat. From this standpoint today's frantic diet-consciousness is a rather good thing. From another standpoint, however, it looks rather hollow. How many of us act on what we have learned about foodstuffs? Some items are fitly called junk food because they are bad for us, yet still we gobble them; other items are rightly called health food because they do us good, yet we pass them by. Are we wise? You tell me.

The story is the same with Christian reading. Many books are written about discipleship, but their quality varies. If we were wise, we would ask which of them are health food as distinct from junk food; but we don't. We buy whatever is there that has a bright cover, a catchy title, and an author's name we have heard before. We deserve to become flabby and short-winded, and so indeed we do, for spiritual muscle and stamina are not developed by Christian junk food.

This book by my colleague Klaus Bockmuehl is health food from start to finish. Assuming that we believe the Gospel of Jesus Christ before we start, it tells us in a clear, no-nonsense, searching way how that Gospel must shape our existence as Christian people. Christian existence is a matter first of receiving love-gifts from a gracious God and then of showing gratitude by tackling tasks that further his glory and others' good, and our own good with both. As eating right is a first step to physical well-being, so thinking right is a first step to spiritual well-being, and this is a right-thinking book. It is not flashy, any more than Granola or eggplant are flashy, but like them it is wonderfully nourishing.

Good health to you!

J. I. PACKER

CONFRONTING
OUR BASIC QUESTIONS

Human life stands in desperate need of courage: the conviction that life will not only continue, but triumph. Without such basic assurance — a reserve of confidence and hope — life withers away, paralyzed by despair.

Many people simply adopt such a confidence, layering it over their lives without ever stopping to ask themselves whether or not it is well-founded. That is recklessness, even impudence.

The Christian faith squarely faces the question of the foundation of our confidence in life and answers it with this declaration: Man does not live by bread alone; man lives by the Word of God, the Gospel. The Good News of Jesus Christ answers the basic questions of our lives: Why is there something and not nothing? How did life come about? Where have we come from? Where are we going?

1

The Gospel for all of life

At first glance, the topic "Living by the Gospel" looks like a treatment of lifestyle, or ethics. Ethics looks at the *conduct* of life. It addresses the question, How should we shape our lives?

Peculiar to humans is this need to conduct life consciously, to think through how to live and what to live for. This requirement demands foresight, perspective, and planning—a process of continual decisionmaking.

It is possible, of course, to drift through life in relative disregard of its demands—at least for a while. But that mode contradicts the nature of human life. We must constantly look for basic provisions; food and shelter do not walk in the front door and announce themselves. For our upkeep alone, conscious action is required.

But there is also the need for a conscious conduct of life in another, deeper sense. The phrase "Living by the Gospel" implies that all human life must constantly draw from a spiritual source. This source is what provides us with the means to go beyond coping, or simply getting by, to overcoming, or living in the courage of our conviction that life will triumph.

The theme "Living by the Gospel" can be interpreted in a twofold manner. It can be understood as referring to the Gospel as the source from which to draw the strength, the means, and the provisions for a life that we consider good and proper. But it can also be understood in a wider sense, as living according to the *standards* of the Gospel. In the first sense, we *receive*; in the second, we *act*. Theologically speaking, the first deals with dogmatics; the second with ethics. We need to look at them together.

Christian ethics never begins from square one, however; it presupposes dogmatics, just as human action is preceded by receiving in many ways. And so we must think about both meanings: 1) the gifts given by the Gospel, and 2) the tasks set by the Gospel; or, *endowments* and *assignments* of the Gospel.

Part One

GIFTS FOR LIFE FROM THE GOSPEL

What are the gifts with which the Gospel endows our lives? This question can, of course, be answered in different ways by different Christians. But some gifts are common to all (although even they are subject to different approaches). The following treatment may seem unusual, but it can serve to remind us of some basic elements of the God-given equipment of the Christian life. I have in mind three gifts of the Gospel: 1) *forgiveness*, 2) *commission*, and 3) a *Counselor*.

1

FORGIVENESS

The Christian Gospel speaks above all about the forgiveness of sins. It is not primarily a revelation for overcoming doubt; it is the Gospel of forgiveness, of Christ and his work, which conquered the sin of humanity. In a prophetic way John the Baptist characterized Jesus and his work: "Behold, the Lamb of God, who takes away the sin of the world" (John 1:29). To this declaration the Christian Church responds, "The blood of Jesus his Son cleanses us from all sin" (1 John 1:7). Sin is the disease; Christ is the cure.

Because it is such a foundational theme, forgiveness easily becomes commonplace—and therefore it may be the first of a whole list of themes we treat superficially and of which we need to regain a more profound understanding. Forgiveness, this gift of the Gospel, is absolutely essential.

Without forgiveness of sin the demand (and desire) for a good and meaningful life must remain impossible to fulfill, considering the moral weakness of humanity. Forgiveness is the only way to keep the brittle tinder, the explosive cancer of evil within us under control. This gift gives to us the purification of our past, the canceling of moral mortgages, the lifting of a load that would otherwise constantly consume our strength. Forgiveness relieves us of the ballast that has accrued in days gone by. It works like the removal of a slab of old concrete from the earth so that natural growth can resume: It enables us to become natural, flexible, free. Forgiveness is the indispensable premise and origin of the much-acclaimed freedom of the Christian.

Forgiveness means that although Christ knows me inside out (John 4:29)—even though he knows that I am not very reliable and not very effective—he does not abandon me. Jesus says, "him who comes to me I will not cast out" (John 6:37), and he underlines this center of his message with the parable of the Prodigal Son. That is an invitation to all, and an invitation that is not bound to the previous fulfillment of any conditions. It may be the most important assurance of our life.

The depth of forgiveness
The depth of God's forgiveness is not easily fathomed. We get a glimpse of it when we begin to understand Christ's death on the Cross in our place. We get an idea of it in the conversion of his

persecutor, the apostle Paul. Paul called himself "a chief of sinners" (1 Timothy 1:15, NKJ), whom, nevertheless, Christ came into the world to save.

This depth of forgiveness matches the depth of our *need* for forgiveness. We need forgiveness for our outright transgression of our Lord's commands, but we also need it for our fickleness and failure, which may do more to hinder Christ's work in the world than the opposition of his declared enemies. Our need of forgiveness is glaringly obvious when we begin to look back on the shabbiness of our performance as Christians, on the lack of sharing and giving where we so richly received. We need forgiveness for the cold love of the years gone by.

Sin is often not so much our active transgression as the good we have knowingly left undone. As the general confession of the Anglican Common Prayer Book puts it, "We have followed too much the devices and desires of our own hearts. . . . We have left undone those things which we ought to have done; and we have done those things which we ought not to have done; and there is no health in us." Indeed, "to him who knows to do good and does not do it, to him it is sin" (James 4:17, NKJ). By that standard, when we are asked for the measure of our loyalty—whether we have loved him with all our heart, with all our soul, and with all our mind (Matthew 22:37)—we stand convicted, and might well react as did the apostle Peter: "Depart from me, for I am a sinful man, O Lord!"

To our conviction and confession of sin, God responds with the great uplifting of forgiveness. This comes out strongly in 1 Corinthians 6:9-11, where Paul lists the deadly sins that exclude a person from entering the Kingdom and then concludes with a striking threefold counterstatement: "Such were some of you. *But* you were washed, *but* you were sanctified, *but* you were justified in the name of the Lord Jesus and by the Spirit of our God." In other words, "where sin abounded, grace abounded much more" (Romans 5:20).

The whole of Scripture supports Paul's testimony to the abundance of God's forgiveness. In the Old Testament, in the midst of the blatant transgression of Israel's idolatry with the golden calf, God himself affirms that he is "merciful and gracious, slow to anger, and abounding in steadfast love and faithfulness" (Exodus 34:6). Man's sin may seem inexcusable. But God is not a justice machine, a device for retribution. He is "full of compassion" and "great in mercy" (Psalm 145:8). With him is "plenteous redemption" (Psalm 130:7), and he will "abundantly pardon" those who turn to him (Isaiah 55:7). In the New Testament, Jesus features the abundance of God's forgiveness in his parable of the wicked servant—"And out of pity for him the lord of that servant released him and forgave him the debt" (Matthew 18:27)—purposely depicting the inequity between what man requested (patience) and what God granted (full pardon). The apostle John, therefore, summed up with all confidence: "The blood of Jesus his Son cleanses us from all sin" (1 John 1:7).

The power of forgiveness

In addition to its liberating effect, forgiveness of sins also has a sobering effect. It wakens us from the dreamy state of living in our illusions and makes us realistic about ourselves. Because of this purifying process, forgiveness of sins is a constant and essential element of Christian humanity.

Forgiveness makes possible the divine establishment and recognition of the individual as person. Whoever denies forgiveness, therefore, may also easily deny the possibility of a personal relationship with God and individual personhood.

This gift of the Gospel, then, accomplishes even more than cleansing our past, or taking us out of the red to a break-even point. It takes us beyond, into the fullness of life itself. To come to Christ means to have life (John 5:40). Jesus himself proclaimed the vigorous, productive power of his forgiveness when he declared, "I am the bread of life; he who comes to me will never go hungry, and he who believes in me will never be thirsty" (John 6:35, NIV).

Living by forgiveness means, first and always, *receiving all that is necessary for living our lives*. It invites us to act out of our receiving. We can trust the reliability and the enduring effectiveness—the lifechanging power—of divine forgiveness.

Not only do we look back into the past in the moment of forgiveness, therefore, but we also look forward into the future. Forgiveness of sins is the mainspring of the Christian life. "I call 'piety,'" declared Calvin, "that reverence joined with love of God which the knowledge of his benefits induces."[1] The motivation of Christian action is *gratitude for forgiveness experienced*. Why? Because gratitude for forgiveness experienced creates love, and love acts so that it pleases the Master. Love for God is the unseen middle link, generated by gratitude for forgiveness. That effect of gratitude also seems to be the meaning of Jesus' word in Luke 7:47 about the woman who was a great sinner: She loved much, because her sins, which were many, were forgiven.

This efficacy of forgiveness has perhaps suffered somewhat by this century's popular interpretation of the Reformational teaching of the justification of the sinner as a strictly declarative statement of God's, comparable to an amnesty, or an acquittal in court—not at the same time a force strong enough to change a person's life, creating a nominal, rather than a real, righteousness.

A passage from the writings of Martin Luther, however, strongly emphasizes the life-changing power of God's gracious forgiveness. No doubt one can pick diverse quotations from Luther's books, and quite divergent theological schools and points of view seem to have made use of him. But the popular interpretation of justification as a static transaction dearly needs to be complemented by

some of the other statements by Luther, such as
his description of the effectiveness of faith:

> . . . that a new man, a new kind and new creation
> comes into being, which is of a quite different
> mind, loves and lives, speaks and works differently
> than before. . . . God's grace is a very strong,
> mighty, and active thing; it does not lie and
> sleep in the soul, as some dream preachers
> imagine, and is not carried around dormant like
> a painted board carries its paint. No, not at all;
> but it is grace that does the carrying; it guides,
> drives, draws, changes and effects everything in
> man—and may indeed be felt and experienced. In
> itself it is hidden, but its works are not.[2]

The necessity of forgiveness

When we link forgiveness to love and Christian
action, we must also reverse this linkage and emphasize, *There can be no truly Christian action
without a personal experience of forgiveness and
love.* This principle seems to be the implication
in the three questions that Jesus put to Peter on
the shores of the Sea of Galilee after his resurrection (see John 21:15-17), when he commissioned Peter to feed his sheep. Three times Jesus
asked Peter, "Do you love me?" Love of Christ
would be the necessary prerequisite to all pas-
toring of Christ's flock. And Peter would be able
to love Jesus only if he understood that even if
his heart condemned him because of his threefold

denial of his Lord, "God is greater than our hearts" (1 John 3:20).

This linkage between Christian action and an experience of forgiveness was also declared necessary by Karl Barth, the great Swiss theologian. With what must be considered a remarkable turning toward a truly biblical theology in the last period of his life, Barth affirmed in his *Church Dogmatics* (in the chapter on vocation to witness) that there can be no Christian witness without a personal experience of salvation. And as every Christian is called to witness, every Christian must necessarily have had that personal experience of salvation before he or she can be a witness in the biblical sense. Knowledge of catechism or dogmatics is not sufficient. Barth illustrates this truth with the parable of a little African boy who, having played for some years with a small wooden lion (or a neat system of theology, Barth adds in an aside directed at his audience of theologians and pastors), was frightened when he encountered the real thing roaring at him.[3] Without such an experience of the reality of the Word of God—which at times is like a roaring lion (Amos 3:8), and at times like a "still small voice" (1 Kings 19:12)—we cannot be true witnesses, and we cannot live the Christian life. Renewal requires forgiveness.

Effective forgiveness, then, is the first gift of the Gospel for our conduct of life. What must we do to receive it? Does God drop it into our lap? Or do we have to work for it?

As we search for an answer, we come across the question that Jesus asked the lame man at the pool of Bethesda. Posed to an invalid who had been lying there for more than thirty years, Jesus' question seems almost offensive: "Do you want to be healed?" (John 5:6). The passive voice, "to be healed," indicates an experience that one must undergo, rather than something that one can effect. Renewal is not a human achievement. Just as the lame man at the pool of Bethesda had no way to bring about his own recovery (thirty-eight years had witnessed to that!), so we, too, have no way to bring about our own healing and the forgiveness of our sin. We must *receive* forgiveness; we must *let it happen to us*. That is why Jesus asks, "Do you *wish* to be healed?" We must desire to be forgiven and restored; we must be willing to let Jesus renew us. This willingness is what Jesus expects of us.

Philip Melanchthon, Luther's close collaborator in the Reformation, again and again (for example, in the Augsburg Confession and its Apology) emphasized that Christ's forgiveness is indeed accessible to all; but it does demand that we "want and accept" the offer.[4]

Is this desire for forgiveness and renewal natural to us, coming so easily that it barely costs us any effort? Perhaps not. We may be too proud to ask for forgiveness, because that request means admitting our own moral and spiritual bankruptcy: It is a commentary on our basic inability to conduct life properly. But effective forgiveness presupposes this honesty about our sin. Through confession, forgiveness becomes realistic. The prodigal son in Jesus' parable is spared from punishment, but not from acknowledging his wrong: "I have sinned against heaven and against you" (Luke 15:21, NIV). This part of the parable points to the spiritual wisdom of spoken confession. Conviction of sin and forgiveness always go together: "A deep sense of sin means a deep sense of Christ."

This need for confession occurs not just once and for all, but continually. Like the two other gifts of the Gospel, commission and counsel, forgiveness must be desired, prayed for, and accepted afresh each day, just as much as we stand in fresh need of it each day.

For in the final analysis, the Christian life—and even human life in general—is impossible without forgiveness. Because it clears the past and reconstitutes life and relationships, forgiveness prevents the stiffening and hardening of the spirit. It keeps us from sclerosis of the character. Ezekiel compared it to replacing a heart of stone with a heart of flesh, which is alive, pulsating, and able to react.

I vividly remember my conversations with the president of the atheist students at a university where I served as a student pastor. Our interchange eventually reached a deep personal level, but this young gentleman stood firm in his rejection of the Christian faith. His denial, however, robbed him of the secret of forgiveness, and his responses to life gradually hardened into rigid and unhappy patterns. He would never, for instance, forgive the girl he had loved, who had been living with him but then had left him for another man, nor would he ever forgive the local policeman who had roughed him up during some student demonstration. He was facing a future crippled by shriveling human relationships which could not be regenerated, like a tree whose dying branches would, in time, drop off one by one.

Forgiveness restores human relationships in every arena of life. The married couple who do not know and practice the secret of daily forgiveness—removing those grains of sand that can bake together over time to build a wall—will almost inevitably end up in divorce. Forgiveness can halt and reverse that process of estrangement. Surely this secret of forgiveness is needed in the same way between parents and children.

This need certainly extends beyond family situations, however. Can you imagine a Christian work, a church, or a mission prospering without forgiveness regularly requested, granted, and received among its members? Without it there would be no check against the constant corrosion of relationships that results from the acid of human sin; hostility and bitterness would build up not only in the heart of the victim, but also in the heart of the perpetrator. In such a situation, work becomes like turning a screw whose threads are stripped—a lot of effort, but no results.

We need God's forgiveness even more. Without it, we easily fall into confusion. We might, for example, be blackmailed into further sin because of our past record—if not by other people, then perhaps even more so by our own heart and by the devil—coercing us into new defeat. With forgiveness we gain a new freedom, confidence, and even lightheartedness, for the essentials of life are now being looked after by the highest Authority.

Forgiveness is effective; it goes hand in hand with God's work of regeneration and rebirth. This is why the believer confesses jubilantly, "He drew me up from the desolate pit, out of the miry bog, and set my feet upon a rock, making my steps secure" (Psalm 40:2). And he quotes God's own words of defiance: "Though your sins are like scarlet, they shall be as white as snow" (Isaiah 1:18). Forgiveness is not a once-in-a-lifetime occurrence, therefore, but the ever-present secret of living. It is to the Christian life what God's constant work of rejuvenation is to creation (see Psalm 104:30). It enables the believer to bounce back from defeat, to rise Phoenix-like from the ashes every time. We may wonder whether there is anything comparable to it in the world of human culture. It is the end to the process of corruption. It gives the lie to determinism. Forgiveness is the key to spiritual advance.

Notes

1. John Calvin, *Institutes of the Christian Religion*, I, 2, 1.

2. Martin Luther, *Works*, Weimar Edition (WA),
    10, I, 1; 113, 15 ff., 114, 20, ff. ("Christmas
    Postil," 1522).
3. Karl Barth, *Church Dogmatics*, Vol. IV, 3, II,
    (Edinburgh: T. & T. Clark, 1962), 647 ff., 658, 660.
4. Philip Melanchthon, "Apology of the Augsburg
    Confession," in *The Book of Concord: The
    Confessions of the Evangelical Lutheran Church*,
    ed. Th. Tappert (Philadelphia: Fortress, 1959), 114.

2

COMMISSION

The second gift of the Gospel is God's *commission* to us. The life-changing power of forgiveness frees us to accept and act on this divine commission. Without effective forgiveness, we wouldn't have the eye or the heart for any concern that went beyond our immediate personal redemption. But once we find a new life in the grace of God, we can move beyond personal preoccupation to enter God's plan for the world.

The fact of commission
Among Karl Barth's many innovative approaches to theology is his rediscovery of an essential aspect of the biblical doctrine of salvation. Barth pointed out that God's saving work for us consists of not only justification and sanctification, as the traditional formula has it, but justification, sanctification,

and *vocation*.[1] We can find the matrix for this tripartite division in the New Testament, where Paul spells out these three categories with remarkable precision in his second letter to Timothy: "You have followed my *teaching*, my *conduct*, and my *aim in life*" (2 Timothy 3:10). Timothy's identification with his mentor meant sharing his doctrine, his practice, and his *prothesis*, or "proposition"— the purpose that had been set before him. To paint a picture of Paul without this particular thrust would be to create a poor representation. Paul was a man with a purpose, and he wanted his younger colleague to follow him in that pursuit.

But many churches miss Paul's emphasis, and they end up with a double deficiency in this area. On the one hand, theologians often limit their efforts to expounding the doctrine of justification "alone." On the other, orthodox believers in the laity devote themselves exclusively to cultivating the great biblical theme of sanctification. The story usually ends here, critically omitting the doctrine of calling and purpose in life. God's work does not come to an end in us as its recipients, however; rather, it is to reach out through us to the whole of humanity. Our calling and commission is to bear witness to God's truth.

We need not look far in the gospels to find Christ's consciousness of his commission, or charge. John 4:34, for example, records this declaration of his calling: "My food is to do the will of him who sent me, and to accomplish his work." Jesus' understanding of himself can be characterized as, "I am an emissary, under orders. *I have been sent.*"

Jesus includes his disciples in this pursuit of his commission: "*We* must work the works of him who sent me, while it is day . . ." (John 9:4). After his resurrection, he passes his own mission on to his disciples, telling them, "Peace be with you. As the Father has sent me, even so I send you" (John 20:21). Jesus' command is that his disciples share his own work.

There are many places in the gospels—the parables, for example—that record Christ's use of the analogy of people who are sent to work (such as into the vineyard) describing those who are sent into God's work. Jesus uses this analogy to emphasize the special nature of the Christian life: We are called and commissioned to cooperate with him in his own work. The Christian's lifestyle is defined by his God-given task—"For we are God's fellow workers" (1 Corinthians 3:9).

God has given us the authority and privilege to act on his behalf, to represent him as plenipotentiary envoys and emissaries; we are "ambassadors for Christ" (2 Corinthians 5:20), and his representatives. Our word *missionary* really has a twofold meaning: Its original sense refers to an envoy, one who is called and sent. Its more specialized sense refers to a messenger who proclaims the Gospel full-time and baptizes new converts. In the original, more general sense, all Christians are missionaries; God calls us, endows us with spiritual gifts, and sends us into ministries.

Christ's affirmation of his commission in John 4:34 shows us that the missionary no longer lives according to his own will, but rather by the will of his Commissioner. The Christian is like a commissioned officer; he has given up his status as a free agent. Paul develops this concept when he compares the Christian to an enlisted soldier who has given up concern for private business or personal development and now seeks to please the one who enlisted him (2 Timothy 2:4).

Commission not only points back to the consciousness of being sent, but also looks forward to the accomplishment of a goal. And here is an important insight into the nature of Christian ethics: In no way does it intend merely the assumption of a new lifestyle, such as modesty and simplicity, but it sets the goal of accomplishing a certain work.

The Greek text of Jesus' statement in John 4:34 emphasizes that it is the Father's work, not his own, that Jesus must complete. This can be a difficult concept for sensibilities trained by our modern age. Think, for example, of the respect and honor we accord the people who submerge personal whim and give themselves to a consistent and ordered life of discipline. We are even more impressed by someone who goes beyond such personal integrity to harness all his abilities in the service of some great creation or contribution—in the arts, in science, in business. Most of us react with awed respect, for example, to Thomas

Mann's sober statement of purpose, which he wrote as a young author to a more lighthearted friend: "Do I care for happiness? I strive after my work."[2] Mann's sense of creating a life work silenced even the all-too-human desire for happiness.

But even Thomas Mann's dedication falls short of the horizon established by Jesus and his disciples. Mann's drive belongs to the philosophy of self-actualization, or self-fulfillment. Jesus and his disciples live for a work that needs to be done, but it does not involve creating their own work. They live to accomplish *God's* work; their concern is the success of *his* mission.

The Church must continually hold before her Christ's declaration of commission: "My food is that I do the will of him who sent me, and accomplish his work." The Church is a purpose oriented fellowship; her task is to proclaim Christ and the Kingdom of God. The Church is called above all to do God's work, not her own. Accomplishing this work is the pivotal point of her entire activity and existence.

Man is created for a life that serves a higher purpose; his existence shrinks away without it. The same holds true for the Church. If she does the will of him who sends her, she will find her food and nourishment, and she will flower and bear fruit. But if she seeks provision for her sustenance elsewhere, she will wither away and die. She exists only to serve her mission.

There was a debate not long ago about whether the Church is above all the vehicle of mission (a functional understanding of the Church) or an entity of which mission is just one task among others. As is often the case in such debates, both sides contain an element of truth. But it is also true that there are those who have found in moments of teamwork in evangelism and service the deepest Christian fellowship, a priceless experience of unity beyond words.

Christ's commission must be central for the Church. Her very nature declares, Here is where the Lord's commission meets with commitment. This commitment is characterized by loving devotion, testifying to Christ's statement that "no one can serve two masters" (Matthew 6:24). Her commitment can never be seen, therefore, as a detached relationship of employment, or a contract spelling out attendance during working hours only, five days a week. "There is no part of our life or conduct, however insignificant," declared Calvin, "which should not be directed to the glory of God."[3] Commission, like forgiveness, is a source of love for and commitment to the Master.

The nature of the commission

But just what is the nature of this work that God calls us to? What are the contents of the Christian's life task?

Christ saw it as his life's work to reconcile humanity to God, which is why we speak of the "high-priestly office" of Jesus. Similarly, Paul describes the essential task of a priest as *bringing people to God* (Romans 15:16). The "priestly service" of the disciples in the New Covenant, then, is the same: to bring people nearer to God. It is the apostolic proclamation of the Gospel, in a manner both extensive and intensive: "Go therefore and make disciples of all the nations, baptizing them in the name of the Father and of the Son and of the Holy Spirit, teaching them to observe everything I have commanded you" (Matthew 28:19-20).

Paul makes a number of striking restatements of this task. What Christ is accomplishing through him is "to lead the Gentiles to obedience to God, by word and deed" (Romans 15:18; cp. 16:26). He emphasizes it again in Colossians 1:28, in what we might call the Pauline parallel to the Great Commission in Matthew 28 (with a similar fourfold emphasis on the universality of the commission): "[Christ] we proclaim, warning every man and teaching every man in all wisdom, that we may present every man mature in Christ Jesus." Paul struggles and directs all his labors to this end, as he states in the next verse. His goal, and the singular passion with which he pursues it, identifies him for all to see with this great theme. He may pursue a variety of means, but his purpose always clearly defines his life.

Another declaration of Christ's, found in John 5:23, also provides insight into our commission. Jesus declares that it is the aim of his work "that all may honor the Son, even as they honor the Father." We can immediately see the parallel between this statement and the first petition of the Lord's Prayer, "Hallowed be your name." This is another definition of the content of the commission. In the final analysis, the commission aims at the fulfillment of the first commandment: "I am the Lord your God. You shall have no other gods before me."

But Christ's phrase in John 5:23 suggests even more about the nature of our mission. He appears to be referring to two stages along the same road— those who already honor the Father will now be brought to acknowledgment and honor of the Son because of the position and purpose given him by the Father. Another passage in John's gospel also points in this direction. Referring to the prophetic promise in Isaiah 54:13, "And they shall all be taught by God," Jesus again pictures this road from the Father to the Son: "Every one who has heard and learned from the Father comes to me" (John 6:45).

In these passages we seem to get a picture of the road taken by the Wise Men from the East, beginning with the study of the stars, on to meditation on the universe of Creation, then through listening to the word of God in the Old Covenant, and finally to the adoration and honor of Jesus. The pagan centurion Cornelius was led along a similar road, from fear of God to personal recognition of his God-sent Savior, Jesus Christ.

To bring people nearer to God, and into fellowship with Christ, is the content of the Christian commission, which we must exercise with all wisdom and in every situation. As the founder of the Prayer Breakfast movement told his young colleagues, in an unforgettable exhortation to this task, "Fan the flame of faith wherever you find it."

The gift of commission

We need to remind ourselves continually that God's commission is a gift of grace to us. Many people will take issue with this concept, objecting, "Isn't a commission a duty you are obliged to discharge, a burden rather than a blessing? Doesn't it drain your strength?" Such an attitude can even be found among Christians — and it reveals a failure to understand the nature of God's commission, even the nature of God himself. It often goes hand in hand with the view — consciously or unconsciously assumed — that God is a tyrant.

In his famous Eleventh Letter, St. Bernard of Clairvaux addressed this attitude when he distinguished between three possible stances toward the divine commission to work. The first stance is that of the slave, who works not because of his own choice, but because of fear of his master. The second is that of a mercenary, who serves merely for a wage, and is primarily concerned with self-interest. St. Bernard acknowledges that it is possible for the motivations of fear and reward to exist in the Christian life in a purified manner to some degree, but this orientation is eclipsed by the third and highest stance — that of the son. The son loves the father, and does whatever his father commissions him to do freely and voluntarily.[4] Jesus perfectly models this stance, and it is what he teaches us to take on. He is clearly motivated not by outward coercion or inward and selfish desire, but by love of God. This love is the impulse of the Holy Spirit, the hidden dynamic of the children of God.

The New Testament reveals that God's commission provides its own inspiration and power; it sustains us. When Jesus says, "My food is to do the will of him who sent me," he is declaring that doing God's will also sustains him physically. He lives by his commission. As the disciples share his commission, the same is true for them. "My food is to do the will of him who sent me" thus becomes an immediate parallel to Christ's charge to his disciples in Matthew 6:33—"Seek first the kingdom of God and his righteousness, and all these things [food and clothing, the strength to love] shall be yours as well." Both these statements of Jesus' support and explain each other.

The commission engenders provision; whoever receives God's commission finds himself richly endowed. "My *food*," Jesus emphasizes, "is that I do the will of him who sent me, and accomplish his work." Whoever accepts this commission will be nourished by it, will live by it, will be perfectly looked after in his needs. When Jesus queried his disciples about the mission he had sent them on, asking, "When I sent you without moneybag, sack, and sandals, did you lack anything?" they replied,

"Nothing." Where God guides, he also provides.

This provision in God's commission reaches yet a deeper level than the supply of material goods, however. God's commission to us grants personal dignity; it creates personality. Once we understand the significance of the commission and our role in carrying it out, we'll learn to "think big" of ourselves—not in terms of who we are or what we bring to the task, but in the context of our goal and calling. Under God's commission can come a remarkable awakening of the gifts and talents in us that had previously lain dormant. Consciousness of commission will bring about a concentration and enhancement of our strength, the harnessing of energies that would otherwise be dissolved or diluted. This infusion of purpose and meaning in life will spur us on to take the initiative. Instead of tagging along for the ride, waiting for others to push or pull us, we'll become self-motivated.

In a time such as ours, which is pervaded by a strong sense of meaninglessness, acquiring such a focus in life has a strongly redeeming quality. Without meaning or purpose, people float aimlessly—a dangerous position to be in, because such aimless drifting is liable to head by default in the direction of the strongest current. Alex Ginsburg, one of the Russian dissidents, recently warned of this same phenomenon observable on a national scale: "You can recognize the inner situation of a country by what people are most occupied with and what they live for. If apathy, selfishness, demands, and banalities dominate in a nation, it can easily slide into a dictatorship."

The commission gives us an identity of our own and an inner independence. It is also of priceless value in relieving us of the all-too-human urge to compare ourselves with others. That urge creates a sense of inferiority and envy, or else superiority and paternalism, all of which are poisonous to teamwork. Paul suggests that instead of comparing ourselves to others, we should try to measure up to our commission: "Let each one examine his own work, and then he will have rejoicing in himself alone, and not in another" (Galatians 6:4, NKJ).

The commission liberates us from drifting and from our natural egocentricity; it boosts us to a different plane of living. Feeding our ego occupies so much of our attention, yet it is so notoriously too small an aim for a human being. Man's creational design is to serve a purpose bigger than his own sustainment. Nonchristians are also aware of this basic need. At a conference in India some years ago, I met an Indian millionaire who had made his fortune in the film industry. When someone introduced me as a theologian, he responded, "Ah, that is interesting. Aren't theologians the people who know all the answers? Tell me what I should do. I have turned fifty. I have made all the money I could ever have dreamed of. I've donated a hospital worth a million dollars to my hometown. But then, people do not love and remember rich men; they only remember good men. [He obviously felt that goodness bought with money was not good enough.] Tell me, what should be my calling for the remaining years of my life?" This man was in search of a true purpose.

Communists seem to be as goal-minded as anyone in our modern world. I have heard one of them describe three particular benefits provided by the Communist system: a perspective of history, a principle of action in the present, and a sense of belonging.[5] I think these three could easily be matched by Christianity; Christians were the first to have a philosophy of history. Unlike the Communists, however, they have an aim that will not soon be devalued again by the course of history, as is the case with most human goals and propositions. Many Communists seem to die disappointed—and for them death is the end of the individual's story; what has not happened by then will not happen to them at all.

In sharp contrast to this earthbound system, the Christian is strengthened in his commission by a hope that goes beyond the visible, beyond all events in space and time. God's commission is thus a priceless gift. We must pray that God would continually give it back to us, as Jesus gave it back to Peter on the shore of the Sea of Galilee after Peter had slipped in his faith: "Do you love me? Feed my sheep" (John 21).

The horizon of the commission

A commission points out a goal that needs to be reached. Here we are at an important crossroads of Christian ethics: It finds its context in a movement toward the future. We have emphasized that God's commission by no means intends merely a new style of living—modesty and meekness, for example—but points to a certain work to be done, and carried to completion. Jesus' concern is to accomplish his Father's work: he looks beyond the current and continuous task of doing God's will to a clearly defined work of God's commission. The horizon of his work gives it its urgency. When Jesus speaks of the completion of God's work, his words remind us that God's charge to us is referring to the future, just as faith generally relates to the future.

Today we must recover the eschatological framework of all our activities. We suffer from what St. Bernard once called a "diffidence regarding the future life."[6] Calvin urged Christians to have a "concern for eternity," an awareness that we now live in preparation, as it were, for the glory of the Heavenly Kingdom. Then we would know how to use this world as if we did not use it (1 Corinthians 7:29-31), and to "bear poverty patiently and abundance with moderation" until the Lord calls us to the glory and peace of his Kingdom.[7]

We must learn afresh to live under the horizon of eternity. This would mean that we "set our house in order" (Isaiah 38:1) and review our priorities. It would mean that we consider our activities in the light of the end of our life, which may come sooner than we think. We must learn to see our present life from the viewpoint of eternity—as a one-time opportunity. Such a perspective will help us guard against accommodating to the fads and opinions of the day, and it will clarify our eternal mission.

This perspective has been almost completely lost to Christianity in the West. Perhaps the reason for this loss is due not so much to the influence of some theological school committed to an existentialist, exclusively here-and-now interpretation of the Gospel, but to our own practical absorption with the immediate interests of the day. Our preoccupation with holding and improving our standard of living—the joys as well as the "worries of this life," as Jesus warned—robs us of the true horizon of our faith. These preoccupations constantly set up their own goals for us. Repugnant theologies follow, to provide theoretical justifications of existing attitudes—another attempt to reconcile practice and theory, only this time on a lower level!

We need to stand against that trend and open our eyes once again to what lies ahead for God's Kingdom. Our charge concerns the future. Only when we grasp this reality again will we understand and take to heart the biblical warning, "Make the most of every opportunity" (Ephesians 5:16, NIV). For the time that is still at our disposal is short.

Our commission is future-oriented. The reverse is also true: The future of God's Kingdom relates to our present commission, and hope becomes a motivation for mission. Whoever has this same hope will wish to participate in the accomplishment of Christ's work.

This expectation of the coming Kingdom is no idle consideration. Its corollary is a warning: Christian hope in the future does not consist of a merely passive attitude of speculation about dates and details, and anticipation of events related to the return of Christ. Nevertheless, again and again there seem to be times when believers think they must occupy themselves with eschatological accountancy and thus get a handle on God's plan of salvation for the future. I recently saw a bumper sticker proclaiming, "Attention! In the event of rapture this vehicle will be without driver." Serious, funny, or improper on both counts?

There is a close connection between this inordinately speculative attention to eschatological events and the contention, sometimes heard today, that "the age of mission is over." This contention denies God's most important commission for the present, and it ends up making reductions of Scripture—just as liberal theology does, drawing criticism from conservatives because of such reductions.

Where, then, should our commission impact the needs of our present age? Knowledgeable and careful observers discern the signs of our times in a comprehensive takeover of power by a secular humanism which denies the authority of God. Secularism, the program of human autonomy, is raising its flag everywhere on our planet. On the other hand, these same observers have identified signs of renewal and reform among Christians. We need not look far to find groups of Christians who have forged a fresh understanding and conviction of their mission and are now looking for ways and means to allow their faith to determine their whole lives.

Both developments, secularism and Christianity, encounter each other today in many places, silently as well as openly. To rescue pockets of humanity from the hands of entrenched atheism in our generation, for the Kingdom of God, may be the perspective with which we have to understand and apply our commission of "accomplishing his work" in our time.

Notes

1. Karl Barth, *Church Dogmatics*, Vol. IV, 1, (Edinburgh: T. & T. Clark, 1956), 145 f.

2. Thomas Mann in a letter to Kurt Martens, dated 28 March 1906: "I am, then, hardly an ascetic, except in the sense: 'Do I strive for happiness? I strive for my work!' I distrust pleasure, I distrust happiness, which I regard as unproductive. I think that nowadays one cannot serve both masters, pleasure and art; that man is not strong and perfect enough to do so. I don't believe that anyone today can be a *bon vivant* and at the same time an artist. One must decide, and my conscience decides for achievement." *Letters of Thomas Mann 1889-1955*, trans. R. & C. Winston (New York: Knopf, 1971), 50. (The quotation is

from F. Nietzsche, *Thus Spake Zarathustra*,
toward the end.) Given changed circumstances,
should the same not be true for Christians?

3. John Calvin, commentary on 1 Corinthians
    10:31; cp. John Calvin, "The First Epistle of
    Paul the Apostle to the Corinthians," *Torrance
    Edition of Calvin Commentaries*, trans. J. W.
    Fraser (Grand Rapids: Eerdmans, 1960), 224.

4. Saint Bernard of Clairvaux, ep. XI, ch. 3;
    cp. *The Love of God and Spiritual Friendship*,
    ed. J. M. Houston (Portland: Multnomah, 1983),
    223 f.

5. Ernst Weiss, in *The Challenge of Marxism*, by
    Klaus Bockmuehl (Colorado Springs: Helmers &
    Howard, 1986), 40.

6. Saint Bernard of Clairvaux (?), *Liber
    Sententiarum*, 117.

7. John Calvin, *Institutes of the Christian Religion*,
    III, 9, 2 f.; III, 10, 4.

3

THE COUNSELOR

The third gift of the Gospel for our lives departs from the nature of the first two in a noticeable way. We are no longer talking of an impersonal concept or truth, but of a person. This endowment is not mere counsel, but a *Counselor*: the Holy Spirit, our God-given advisor. Because of his presence we can know not only our commission, but also the appropriate means to carrying out that commission.

This activity of a divine advisor is mentioned, among other places, in the messianic prophecy of Isaiah 9:6—"For to us a child is born, to us a son is given; and the government will be upon his shoulders. And his name will be called Wonderful Counselor, Mighty God, Everlasting Father, Prince of Peace."

Many of us are familiar with this passage because we have heard it read at Christmas services or have had to memorize it for Sunday school or confirmation class. But how many of us have studied it in any detail? It reveals a dimension of God's role as Counselor that we miss in a casual reading. The Latin version of Scripture, the Vulgate, translates this verse with stronger wording: "*datus est nobis . . . consiliarius fortis*"—meaning a counselor such as kings would have. This statement, however, seems paradoxical because it carries the sense of an advisor with power to implement his advice. The Counselor is enabler as well as advisor; he gives us strength as well as counsel. "Great are your purposes and mighty are your deeds," Jeremiah exclaims to the Lord after experiencing his clear guidance in purchasing the land at Anathoth (Jeremiah 32:19).

Isaiah mentions this gift in many other places. Isaiah 11:2, for example, which contains the promise that led to the traditional Christian doctrine of the seven gifts of the Holy Spirit (wisdom, understanding, counsel, strength, knowledge, godliness, fear of the Lord), speaks of "the Spirit of counsel." And passages appearing later in the book of Isaiah indicate that this special gift follows from the very nature of God. The God of Israel says of himself, "This is what the Lord says—your Redeemer, the Holy One of Israel: 'I am the Lord your God, who teaches you what is best for you, who directs you in the way you should go'" (Isaiah 48:17, NIV). God offers himself to his people as teacher, counselor, and guide: "Whether you turn to the right or to the left, your ears will hear a voice behind you, saying, 'This is the way; walk in it'" (Isaiah 30:21, NIV).

We can look at the instructions for the Christian life as a framework composed of the Ten Commandments, their exposition in the general category of scriptural exhortation, plus the "wisdom from above" spoken of in James 1:5. The commandments form the basic order; our conscience serves as an individualized and internalized moral law, pointing out the truth and our condition relative to it (cf. Romans 9:1).

The general guidelines of the Law—the commandments—are certainly a precious gift from God. But in addition to them, God also grants situational directives. The psalms as well as the prophets proclaim this specific gift from the Lord, as in Psalm 32:8—"I will instruct you and teach you in the way you should go; I will counsel you and watch over you" (NIV).

Surprisingly, Psalm 119—often understood, perhaps wrongly, only as referring to the written law revealed in the distant past—seems to speak of this very experience of situational guidance. The frequently occurring Hebrew term *choq* (e.g., 119:5) also means the actual command by which, for example, the leader leads a group, or with which a ruler directs the nation in war or peace (cf. Judges 5:9, "the commanders of Israel," and Isaiah 33:22, "the Lord is our ruler"), and not merely timeless "statutes." It is something that God may even yet have to teach, and thus something for which we can pray (see Psalm 119:26).

Another Hebrew term frequently used in Psalm 119 that is often translated in a static and unspecific manner as "commandments," or "statutes," really has the connotation of concrete, individual communication: *piqudim* (e.g., 119:4) denotes "commissions, charges, appointments."

Psalm 119:26 also offers another phrase for the same continual communication: "When I told of my ways, thou didst answer me." This sense is echoed in the New Testament in Luke 2:26, where we learn that Simeon "had received an answer by the Holy Spirit" that he would see the Messiah before he died (cf. Romans 11:4 as well). Psalm 119:24 actually uses the word "counselor"—"Your testimonies are my delight, they are my counselor."

A commission entails orders, but the Christian life transforms this image with a new meaning. Jesus addressed this change, which follows a change in relationship: "No longer do I call you servants, for the servant does not know what his master is doing; but I have called you friends, for all that I have heard from my Father I have made known to you" (John 15:15). In addition, he promised them the Holy Spirit, "another helper" (John 14:16) who, in his own absence (14:26), would "teach them all things" and lead them into "all the truth" (John 16:13).

The term "counsel" seems to go beyond orders or commands; it carries a sense of option about it.

It works through nonbinding suggestions that are not forced upon us, but rather leave the decision up to us. We could compare the term "counselor" to our contemporary concept of "the consultant." Today's business world is full of consulting firms; the Holy Spirit is the consultant to whom Christians are to turn for advice and guidance. Then the experience and prayer of the psalmist will be true again for us: "The unfolding of thy words gives light; it imparts understanding to the simple" (Psalm 119:130). This kind of counsel seeks to convince, not command. How much more necessary it is, therefore, that we listen!

The New Covenant considers this gift of counsel and guidance essential, because the guidance of the Spirit is the basic presupposition and precondition for the New Testament freedom in Christ, and for the mellowing of the Law that was formerly deadly. "If you are led by the Spirit, you are not under the law" (Galatians 5:18). That statement of Paul's should settle the issue once and for all: The indwelling of the Holy Spirit is the prerequisite to Christian freedom because, according to Romans 8:4, the Holy Spirit himself will look after the fulfillment of the legitimate demands of God's law.

It is Jesus who offers this gift of the Spirit to the people he encounters. Thus he tells the semipagan woman at the well of Samaria, "If you knew the gift of God, and who it is that asks you for a drink, you would have asked him and he would have given you living water" (John 4:10, NIV).

God freely gives his Holy Spirit through the hand of Jesus; all it takes is asking—"If you, then, though you are evil, know how to give good gifts to your children, how much more will your Father in heaven give the Holy Spirit to those who ask him!" (Luke 11:13, NIV). Moreover, "God gives the Spirit without limit" (John 3:34, NIV), "abundantly" (Titus 3:6), like his forgiveness—not meagerly or strictly measured, but like "living water" from a running source, constantly available and always fresh.

Divine guidance is, however, a matter of humility and patience. Psalm 106:13 says of the Israelites, "They soon forgot [God's] works, they did not wait for his counsel." Divine guidance is a gift that requires two things: remembering earlier experiences with the Lord, and waiting—i.e., patience. It thus demands memory and perseverance. These two are always the ingredients of faith; faith looks both into the past and toward the future (see Matthew 16:9 and Hebrews 11).

The forgotten gift of the Spirit
God finds it difficult to present us with gifts. His gift of forgiveness too often meets with closed hands; man's pride does not allow him to admit that he cannot accomplish his own cleansing himself. Similarly, the gift of the divine commission finds few people ready and grateful; far too many have already accepted other commissions or set up their own goals, and God's commission becomes just one more, and one too many. It is also

true that not a few Christians receive God's forgiveness and then simply continue to follow their own intentions. They never move on to God's commission to service. They want to be saved, but they don't want to serve.

The situation is even more problematic, however, when it comes to the gift of the Counselor, the Holy Spirit.

The story of Israel clearly illustrates man's problem with accepting the gift of God's divine guidance. Hardly is the Spirit promised when the people begin a tenacious struggle to block and evade his commission and his ministry. They are only too ready, in fact, to follow other plans and counsel: "'Woe to the rebellious children,' says the Lord, 'who carry out a plan, but not mine; and who make a league, but without my Spirit; who set out to go down to Egypt, without asking for my counsel!'" (Isaiah 30:1 ff.).

Elijah, a prophet commissioned by God, had already spoken sternly to one of the leaders of Israel about this very issue: "Is it because there is no God in Israel that you are going to inquire of Baal-zebub, the god of Ekron?" (2 Kings 1:3). Now, in this later situation that Isaiah describes, they again seek counsel and support from Egypt, a nation that cannot help them, instead of from "the spirit of wisdom and understanding, the spirit of counsel and might" (Isaiah 11:2).

Like Israel, the Church has often enough tried to obtain the wisdom it needs from somewhere other than God—from pagan philosophies, for example. But these other apparent resources are actually "broken cisterns, that can hold no water" (Jeremiah 2:13). In contrast to the "rebellious children" that God spoke of through the prophet Isaiah, "loyal children" are those who ask for God's counsel, carry out his plans, seek refuge with his Spirit. Only then are they true children of God, if they follow in the footsteps of their father Abraham, who obeyed God's command from day to day. They are true children of God if they emulate young King Solomon, who asked God to give him a "listening heart" (1 Kings 3:9, in the Hebrew text—instead of "understanding mind," the misguided translation frequently used). The "cisterns" of those who look to the Lord will be filled to overflowing.

The best tradition of the Church has always held that it is "in quietness and silence that man becomes prudent" (St. Bernard). It takes silence to listen to the divine Counselor. Isaiah declared in respect to this same theme, "in quietness and in trust shall be your strength" (Isaiah 30:15). This and similar verses are often given a prominent place in the life of a church, and they may even be turned into a kind of watchword for a year or two. Their context, however, which alone reveals their true meaning, is often neglected. The opposite of bewildered helplessness is not sitting quietly in stoic inactivity, but the quality of quietness filled with inquiring prayer and a listening heart.

In his exposition of the third commandment (of the year 1525), Martin Luther powerfully characterized this attitude of expectant waiting:

> Thus the holy people carefully saw to it that they
> on no account would undertake anything unless
> they first were certain that God undertook
> it in them. However, when they were uncertain
> they kept still with saying and singing and doing.
> This is the true manner of Sabbath—which all
> the world has forfeited, and accepted the Devil's
> observance instead.[1]

Luther's judgment may seem severe, but it may well have been justified when his time is held up against the example set by the saints and fathers of the early Church. It is obvious that much of modern Protestantism falls under the same judgment. Large sections of Protestantism today have simply forgotten about the Holy Spirit. Since the end of the last century, liberal theology has rejected any idea of an immediate, personal communion between the believer and God. Its representatives have sneered at what they call an "imaginary private relationship with God."[2] And there is a similar tendency within the orthodox Protestant camp: they maintain that the outpouring of the Holy Spirit at Pentecost was a one-time-only event, the same as Christ's crucifixion and resurrection. These events are indeed described in Scripture as having taken place *ephapax*, or once-and-for-all. The outpouring of the Spirit, however, is not reduced to that first occurrence on the day of Pentecost (Acts 2), as the Acts of the Apostles already intimate when they relate a second such episode (Acts 4).

The orthodox are always the guardians of doctrine. But under their superintendence, the doctrine of the Spirit has become static. Primarily, the Spirit occurs in their teaching only as the third person in the doctrine of the Trinity, accompanied by definitions of his nature and his relationships within the Godhead. In better theology textbooks, he is discussed as the true interpreter of Scripture. Very little seems to be said, however, about the rest of his work—such as his actions in regenerating, sanctifying, enabling, inspiring, and instructing the believer. Where this reduction of the doctrine of the Holy Spirit's work exists, it is no wonder that the idea of love for God also falls by the wayside.

What is unfortunately true of liberals and orthodox alike can also be found in evangelicalism. To many evangelicals the Holy Spirit is a stranger, and his annual day of remembrance an awkward occasion. For many years now I have heard evangelical sermons that turned Pentecost into a celebration of fellowship and the Church, along the lines of the Old Testament Feast of Weeks, in a skillful circumnavigation of the Holy Spirit and his work of counseling and enabling.

Perhaps the same reason underlies our long-standing custom of translating *parakletos*, the Greek New Testament title of the Holy Spirit, primarily as "Comforter" and rarely as "Counselor." The latter meaning is just as present in the Greek term as the former. We seem to be able to manage without the divine Counselor.

An ignorance or neglect of the Holy Spirit's task of directing the believer permeates liberal, Reformed orthodox, and evangelical camps. In all three groups, it is a well-known phenomenon that one virtually plans one's life with a strong will of one's own. That inward quietness and restraint before action, which Luther described as the particular quality of the saints, disappears—along with the attitude of listening for the instructions of the Holy Spirit. One of the consequences of this major omission is mediocrity: the absence of creativity, of new form, of surprise. It is the price of our failure to pay attention to the instruction of the Spirit.

This failure is part of our practical atheism: In many of our daily decisions, we seem to have no need for God, and in fact live without him. Isaiah's prophetic record of God's condemnation of Israel, "they do not ask for my counsel" (Isaiah 30:2), can just as well be said of us. But then we also lack an adequate answer to the claims of *theoretical* atheism—such as the "death of God" movement—when it or some other secular ideology captures the spirit of our practical defection in its theory and doctrine.

What Protestantism as a whole needs today is the pursuit, rediscovery, and renewal of spirituality—life in the Spirit. Currently, this field of study has little room in the Church, or in the edifice of theology, or in the syllabi of seminaries, evangelical and orthodox alike.

A time of theological controversy such as ours seems to consume major energies in the defense of doctrinal purity. So some spend all their time defending doctrine, while others dive into evangelism and missions, and still others commit themselves to urgent social concerns. What these groups often fail to realize, however, is that when the spiritual life atrophies, all other labors are doomed to fail.

We must find our way back from our multitude of activities to quiet, and more quiet, to prayer and profound Bible study, to communion with Christ, to listening to the powerful Counselor who has been given to us.

This perspective is endorsed by the witness of two men who in their time were aware of these same needs in Protestantism. One of them, Gerhard Tersteegen, was a Christian layman, a ribbon-weaver by trade, and perhaps the best-known representative of Reformed (Calvinist) Pietism in Germany. This man, who helped many find the road to eternal life, would advise Christians struggling with anxiety,

> You've got so many things to say to God:
> this is what you wish, that is your complaint.
> Make room for him, be silent for a while,
> and listen to what he says and what he would
> have from you.

Oh, people seek so many things and never
find enough;
I am content, because I seek but one.
Their labors are abundant, mine is a single work:
how I might hear in quiet what Jesus has to say.[3]

The other testimony comes again from Martin
Luther. In his remarkable pamphlet, "To Master
Peter Barber, How to Pray" (1535), Luther gives
insight into his own experience of prayer. He describes what listening prayer, conversation with the
Holy Spirit, looks like in practice. Here is his description of how he uses the Lord's Prayer:

> It often happens that I find myself with such rich
> thoughts in one petition of the Lord's Prayer that
> I let all the six petitions wait. When such rich
> good thoughts come, one should let the other
> prayers go and give room to these thoughts, listen
> in silence and by no means hinder. For here the Holy
> Spirit himself is preaching, and one word of his
> sermon is better than thousands of our own prayers.

Later on in this piece Luther observes that we
might find the same experience while praying
through the Ten Commandments:

> As I said above about the Lord's Prayer, I
> encourage you again: If the Holy Spirit should
> come with all those thoughts and begin to preach
> into your heart with rich and illuminating

thoughts, then do him the honor, let your own
ideas go, be quiet and listen to him who can
do it better than you, and take note of what
he preaches and write it down and you will see
miracles, as David says, in God's law.
(Psalm 119:18)[4]

The intention of the Counselor

We must not conclude this section on the gift of
the divine Counselor without having said something about the purpose and intention of this gift,
according to Scripture. The instruction by the Spirit
is the actualization of the divine commandments
into our current situation. It is a gift *of the Gospel*.
Thus it will always take its place within the framework of God's law and Gospel—not outside of it.
Moreover, it is a *gift for service*. The divine Counselor acts on the basis of forgiveness and interprets
the divine commission. Above all, the Holy Spirit
is given in support of missions—that is the message
of John 20:21-22. The Holy Spirit advises and leads
the advance of missions.

This correspondence of guidance and ministry
is already expressed in the Old Testament by
Isaiah, in one of the weightiest passages this
prophet has on the subject of divine instruction.
He says in chapter 50, verse 4: "The Lord God has
given me the tongue of those who are taught, that
I may know how to sustain with a word him that
is weary. Morning by morning he wakens, he
wakens my ear to hear as those who are taught."

These statements emphasize the closest possible correlation between proclamation and a preceding divine instruction. Whoever will speak to man must first listen to God. They also emphasize a regularity of divine tuition; the original Hebrew text even expresses this sense structurally, with the repetition *baboker, baboker*—"in the morning, in the morning," meaning "morning by morning." The divine direction is not a rare event, such as the movement of the waters in the pool of Bethesda, which would become curative only at unpredictable moments and so infrequently that a person might remain without the healing touch of God's power for almost forty years (see John 5:4 ff.). No, Isaiah had already experienced the regularity and permanence of the gift that Jesus promised his disciples (John 14) and put into effect for the whole membership of the Church on the first day of Pentecost: the gift of the Holy Spirit, who guides us into all truth (John 16:13) and who abides with us (1 John 2:27).

The gift of divine direction wholly serves the purpose "that I may know how to sustain with a word him that is weary." The guidance of the Spirit does not come first for our own comfort or pleasure; rather, it comes to help sustain our neighbor. People do get tired and weary and need to be strengthened. This sustenance is to happen with a "word," merely a simple, unobtrusive word—but one that has its source in God and is therefore effective.

Without the "Divine Teacher," as the early Church called the Holy Spirit, we do not know how to spiritually uphold the life of our weary neighbor. As feeble humans ourselves, we do not have it in us to revive and sustain The divine Counselor is indispensable in this situation; otherwise, we end up trying to run the show, and even Christianity, ourselves. Human reason, or even "illumined human reason," as some claim, may indeed be appropriate for decision-making in the realms of creational ethics and civil vocation. But as soon as we face the exigencies of God's Kingdom in the order of salvation, we need to have not only the goal but also the means given to us. If we fail to ask for them, our performance will be like a suit that doesn't fit—it's no good for the customer.

Availing ourselves of the means to reach our God-given goal takes, as Isaiah says, a separate act of waking our ears, which precedes listening, just as listening precedes knowing, and knowing precedes the word and action of our support for others. On their own, our ears seem to be closed or asleep. They must be opened for the instruction of the Spirit.

This divine guidance is the third great gift of the Gospel for our conduct of life, next to forgiveness of sins and commission—the Counselor, the Holy Spirit. With different but no less biblical imagery, Count Zinzendorf, the eminent leader of the Moravian Brethren, reflected this promise of the Gospel in one of his hymns:

God's Love will guide us, prepare the road,
and point to many things just with her eyes:
whether't be time to fight or time to rest.
Love will prepare us, e'en in these times.
Let *us* be faithful.[5]

Notes

1. Martin Luther, WA, 16, 483, 12 ff. ("Sermons on the Ten Commandments," 1524/1527).
2. W. Herrmann, following A. Ritschl, in *The Communion of the Christian with God*, ed. R. Voelkel (Philadelphia: Fortress, 1971), 210. 285n.
3. Gerhard Tersteegen, *Leben heiliger Seelen*, Bd. 1, Lahr 1960, 35 ff.
4. Luther, WA, 38, 363, 9 ff.; 366, 10 ff. ("A Simple Way to Pray, for a Good Friend," 1535).
5. Count Zinzendorf, in *Gesangbuch der ev.-ref. Kirchen der deutschsprachigen Schweiz* (Evangelical Hymnal of German-speaking Switzerland), 322:2.

Part Two

TASKS ARISING FROM THE GOSPEL

In the first part of this book, we explored "Living by the Gospel" in terms of "living by the power that God holds out through the Gospel." We discovered three major gifts of the Gospel that empower our lives: forgiveness, commission, and the Counselor.

In the second part of this book, we'll look at our subject in terms of "living by the directions and standards set by the Gospel." Which tasks are paramount as we seek to make the Gospel of Jesus Christ the sole foundation for our lives? Among the many activities and pursuits called forth by this Gospel, at least three seem especially crucial: 1) prayer, 2) sustainment and preservation; and 3) the proclamation of the Gospel.

All Christian action, of course, comes under the Gospel's "double commandment of love"—love of God and love of neighbor (Matthew 22:37-40). One of the first expressions of love of God is prayer.

4

PRAYER

Prayer is a sign of life, and it commands first place among the human activities and tasks initiated by the Gospel. It is a natural manifestation of life in Christ: we pray the moment we become Christians, and we must continue it all along our subsequent walk of serving our Lord.

The Gospel points to an apparent paradox in this area: the seemingly passive task of prayer is to have a prime role in the life of an active Christian. Our precedent for this paradox is the life of Jesus: The first few chapters of John's gospel give us a picture of Christ's continual immersion in this vital communion. John 6:15 records, ". . . Jesus withdrew again to the mountain by himself." Again and again, Jesus sought solitude in order to speak with God. His life was composed with the two-stroke rhythm of solitary silence and public activity.

For Jesus, prayer is not dialogue with men, but conversation with God.

The Greek term employed in some of these passages is *monos*, "alone" (twice also in Matthew 14:23). This same root later gave rise to the name of the "monk"—that is, the solitary one—and of monastic life as a separate lifestyle. The Reformation attacked monasticism at this very point, as the repudiation of all human society.

We must not respond to one extreme, however, with the opposite extreme. We cannot simply surrender the solitude of prayer. Especially in today's generation of activism and collectivism, we need to defend and maintain separate times for individual communion with God.

The right balance lies in the Gospel, which takes yet a third position beyond separation or collectivism. It teaches that although solitude is a necessary element of the Christian life, it is not an estate of its own. Proclamation and service on the one hand, and prayer on the other, are part and parcel of the same life—not to be distributed to two different groups of people. The two elements relate to each other in differences of times and seasons, not in differences of people.

This two-stroke rhythm may also be the solution to the age-old problem of antithesis between individual and community, just as it represents the fulfillment of the double commandment of love for God and love for neighbor.

It is this personal, individual prayer that we must especially deal with. "Blessed are those who seek him with their whole heart" (Psalm 119:2). Prayer is the practical manner of seeking the face of God. It is man's request that God might speak, and it is man's answer to God's speaking.

Here is the connection between this gift of the Gospel and that of the Holy Spirit as the divine Counselor. "Whosoever prays, calls the Holy Spirit to come," wrote St. Bernard of Clairvaux.[1] Prayer opens the way to receiving instruction and counsel from the Holy Spirit; it is confidential conversation with God.

We are Christians to the degree that we continually enter into dialogue with Christ, that we stop in our whirl of activities and ask, What is God's will? Where does his commission point us? We spoke earlier of our practical atheism—the failure to seek God's counsel, like the "rebellious children" of Israel in Isaiah 30 who did not ask for God's counsel and made their decisions without God's Spirit. Reliance on God does not mean forfeiting our initiative and drifting in passive expectation, but actively petitioning God for his specific instruction: What is his plan for this day, and for the current stage of our pilgrimage?

In prayer we can clarify the specific aims of our commission. Dialogue with God opens up our perspective. In this communion some of the great men and women of God have been given glimpses of his glory. We answer God's commission in prayer, the act of human commitment: "Here I am; send Thou me."

Prayer is also the receptacle for the first gift of the Gospel we looked at, forgiveness. Those who ask for this gift receive it anew, again and again. The church fathers have advised structuring prayer especially around some of the petitions of the Lord's Prayer—for example, "Forgive us our trespasses," "Give us this day our daily bread," and "Hallowed be your name." Perhaps we need to learn to pray as specifically about our needs for forgiveness—and the hallowing of God's name— as about our daily needs for personal provision.

In Psalm 51, the three elements of prayer figure prominently: forgiveness, restoration of our commission, and the presence and guidance of the Holy Spirit. Prayer cleanses and refreshes the heart, clarifies our inner life, and consequently allows the soul to breathe more easily. "The beginning, and even the preparation, of proper prayer is the plea for pardon with a humble and sincere confession of guilt," said Calvin. "It is no wonder that believers open for themselves the door to prayer with this key."[2]

It is often true that where there is spiritual exhaustion and defeat, there is the absence or lack of prayer. This neglect disables our spiritual life as lack of oxygen suffocates our physical life. Prayer, or communion with Christ, brings us back to spiritual health, neutralizing the constant assault of temptation like a powerful disinfectant at work against germs.

When these temptations of our modern world—whether of sex, success, money, or a host of others—threaten to destroy us, prayer restores us with the strength to stand against them. Where there is prayer, there is stability and trustworthiness. Much of human life today is characterized by emotional bankruptcy—the result of a desperate and often futile search for peace and some degree of inner equilibrium. The only way we can survive this raging turbulence, and provide some resting place for others, is by constant retreat to prayer. Only when we know the immovable point of reference can we step out confidently and make bold decisions. A shrewd observer noted this truth in the midst of the destruction and turmoil of World War II: "In situations where the cleverest fail and the most courageous try to retreat, one sometimes sees a man quietly give good counsel and do the right thing. One can be sure that that is someone who prays."[3]

In addition to its power to stabilize, over time prayer will also discipline, civilize, and educate. Prayer makes a person teachable; it creates a general attitude of flexibility. It fosters spiritual alertness and a willingness to be taught by the Holy Spirit. *Prayer shapes our personality*.

The gifts of the Gospel for our lives—forgiveness, commission, counsel—are received by the open hands of prayer, realized by the dynamic of this intimate communion. Melanchthon rightly called prayer the surest sign of distinction of the true Church of Christ.[4]

Prayer is also the first tool for our tasks, the primary weapon of our battle in sanctification, service, and witness. It goes before us like the trumpet blasts around the town of Jericho, crumbling the obstacles that stand in our way. Prayer prepares the way for action, whether our task be missions, evangelism, or service.

Without prayer, it would be senseless for us to engage in the struggle for the completion of God's work in the world. We can claim that we are in the middle of spiritual warfare, but that battle is mere make-believe until it becomes real through intense prayer. Armed only with human weapons, our threat is ridiculous to the powers of evil. As we call upon God, however, forces of another size and quality come into play, and our struggle becomes serious. It will not be without effect in history.

We must recognize that prayer is not only a natural outworking of the Christian life, but something that is positively commanded by God. In his *Large Catechism*, Luther interpreted the second commandment ("You shall not take the name of the Lord your God in vain") as the commandment to pray. He drew the consequence, "Prayer, therefore, is as strictly and solemnly commanded as all the other commandments, such as having no other gods, not killing, not stealing, etc."[5] An understanding of prayer is therefore a necessary part of Christian ethics, the doctrine dealing with the Christian conduct of life.

The promise of prayer

Prayer has the divine promise of being heard. All of Scripture supports invitation and exhortation to prayer. It provides us with a concept of God that emphasizes his presence and accessibility. God is *approachable*. He characterizes himself as one who speaks—"Here I am" (Isaiah 52:6)—as one who hears prayers and answers invocation. He is quite different from the mute idols of the heathen. He wants us to understand that above all, he is the God who answers prayer. "He is not far from each one of us," Paul declared (Acts 17:27).

In the debates of the early Church a pagan challenged a Christian, "I will give you a drachma, if you show me where God is." Replied the Christian, "And I will give you two, if you show me where he is not." God is everywhere. The God of the Gospel is not merely the omnipresent one, however, who as such might remain silent and practically inaccessible to the calls of humans. The true God has, once and for all, proven his presence—his pledge "Here I am"—by his incarnation in Jesus Christ his Son, the Immanuel ("God with us"). He still proves his special presence through the Holy Spirit with those who are his, according to his promise: "Lo, I am with you always, even to the close of the age" (Matthew 28:20).

That promise is something that we need to "cash in on" far more than we do. Western Christianity today seems in general to suffer from a poverty of prayer. If there were more prayer, the world would look different. We must explore the possibilities of prayer more deeply, "for the eyes of the Lord are upon the righteous, and his ears are open to their prayer" (1 Peter 3:12).

Correspondingly, the Bible encourages fearless and demanding prayer. One of the most profound words of Jesus in this respect is found in the parable of the persistent friend. Jesus designed his parable so that it begins with the words, "Which of you has a friend . . ." (Luke 11:5). He wants to make the point that we may confidently approach God with our petitions because in him we have nothing less than a friend.

An incident in the life of Jesus, the healing of a Roman centurion's servant, is in effect another parable of God's willingness to respond to prayer. The centurion had petitioned Jesus with full confidence in his ability and willingness to help. So when Jesus said, "Go; be it done for you as you have believed" (Matthew 8:13), we must of course add, "and as you have asked." Jesus fulfilled the centurion's request, according to the divine rule he gave regarding our requests of the Father: "If you then, who are evil, know how to give good gifts to your children, how much more will your Father who is in heaven give good things to those who ask him!" (Matthew 7:11). The gift is there for the asking. God is serious when he declares, "Here I am."

On the other hand, the respective human response, "Here I am" (1 Samuel 3, Isaiah 6), by which man puts himself at God's disposal, is also a necessary part of prayer. Any honest prayer is based on this presupposition. Prayer demands of us an attitude of devotion and commitment; we must, after all, come to God with open hands.

Serious prayer must be preceded by the rejection and removal of our accrued idols, our pet ideas, and our prized possessions, which captivate our attention and commitment for themselves. These false gods, which may include not only ideas, but also people—a man, a woman, a child—at times so demand precedence over God that they practically paralyze our prayer, dislodging our desire for God. However, God alone is worthy of fundamental and final commitment.

Christ's instructions about how to approach God at the altar ("If you are offering your gift at the altar, and then remember that your brother has something against you, leave your gift there and go; first be reconciled"—Matthew 5:23 ff.), when applied in a general sense to prayer, teach us that disruptions in our human relationships also disrupt the peace and innocence of our relation to God. Here again we must prepare the path of prayer.

The content of prayer
We have God's promise that when we speak, he

hears. But what is to be the substance of our speaking? Here we enter into the content of prayer: praise and thanksgiving, confession, petition, and intercession.

Martin Luther recommended that we begin our time of prayer with thanksgiving, for, he felt, "Thanksgiving and a reminder of God's goodness makes prayer courageous and strong. Otherwise it is heavy, lazy and cold, if the heart is not previously inflamed with the coals of kindnesses received."[6] We need to pause to give thanks to God for creation as well as salvation. Repeated times of "counting our blessings," recalling what we so easily forget, will give us a completely different outlook on life.

Thanksgiving is not merely the fuel for other prayer, however; thanksgiving and praise of God becomes an act of worship, an end in itself: "Save us, O Lord our God," exclaimed Israel, "and gather us from among the nations, that we may give thanks to thy holy name and glory in thy praise" (Psalm 106:47).

Confession of sin is another preeminent element of prayer. It is a necessary corollary of any prayer for forgiveness, and thus stands at the very gate of the Christian life. If there is one condition for forgiveness of sins, it is confession. Three psalms especially emphasize this theme: 25, 32, and 51. Confession is the act of *acknowledging our sins before God* (Psalm 32:5), instead of hiding, excusing, and defending them. It requires that we "call a spade a spade" by expressly admitting what we have done wrong. We may wish to cover up our sinful state, even with a religious disguise, but God wants to see honesty rule our relationship with him. Confession of sins implies telling God that *he* is right; it is another form of acknowledging his kingship and rule.

How do we acknowledge our sins before God? Our confession can include sins of thought, word, and action. The psalmist identified sins of weakness and confusion, as well as acts of conscious disobedience and rebellion against God. We should also remind ourselves that next to the sins of *commission* there are those of *omission*—our failure, our forgetfulness, the wastelands of irrelevance in our lives which we may not easily recognize but which we must ask God to reveal to us. We sin whenever we fail to live up to our commission and calling, in everything that detracts from honoring God's name, and in the expressions of our passive and active selfishness, as we seek our own and deny his rule. Taken seriously, the double commandment of love for God and neighbor is a clear mirror for confession, and it will reflect those areas in which we need to declare ourselves sinners and seek cleansing and restoration.

The prayer of petition is to be just as concrete as thanksgiving and confession; it must deal with palpable objects. "A person who wants to pray," Luther says in his *Large Catechism*, "must present a petition, naming and asking for some things which he desires. Otherwise it cannot be called a prayer."[7] The prayer of petition is the channel through which we present our needs to God and ask that he would look after them—it is like handing them over to him to deal with. Making such a request and then taking the needs back to worry over is no good. Our choice is either to worry or to pray. Prayer replaces anxiousness; it "consumes fear." Paul's counsel is: "Let your gentleness be known to all men. The Lord is at hand. Be anxious for nothing, but in everything by prayer and supplication, with thanksgiving, let your requests be made known to God" (Philippians 4:5-6, NKJ). And then let go!

Some of us must learn this letting go regarding material provisions. We need to pray sincerely, "Give us our daily bread and clothing and a place to live"—all the necessary things Jesus speaks of in Matthew 25:31-46. Others may have to learn to replace anxiety in air travel with prayer, and continually learn it afresh. Desire to receive must be turned into request, because of God's promise to hear and to give, and because of past experience of God's succor. Prayer is a sign of faith; and only faith has the promise of receiving.

Some people have difficulty with the idea of petitionary prayer. Prominent Protestant theologians in the nineteenth century set up veritable barriers between believers and the prayer of petition. For them, making requests of God seemed awkward and inappropriate, because it was tantamount to asking God to redirect the course of the world for man's sake. The God of liberal theology was not expected to do things like that. He was very much distant and sublime, and not the pal that the Pietists depicted. Consequently, only the prayer of thanksgiving was appropriate.

The Reformers had no use for such limitations on approaching God. Luther not only defended petitionary prayer, he even demanded—with his customarily colorful language—that it be courageous and substantial. After all, he reasoned, those who pray present their concerns to the King of kings and Lord of lords! Thus Luther declared,

> Because God is God, he claims the honor of giving far more abundantly and liberally than anyone can comprehend—like an eternal, inexhaustible fountain which, the more it gushes forth and overflows, the more it continues to give. He desires of us nothing more ardently than that we ask many and great things of him; and on the contrary, he is angered if we do not ask and demand confidently.

Luther underlines his exhortation with a brilliant illustration that gives us a glimpse of God's great generosity:

> Imagine a very rich and mighty emperor who bade a poor beggar to ask for whatever he might desire, and was prepared to give great and

princely gifts, and the fool asked only for a dish of beggar's broth. He would rightly be considered a rogue and a scoundrel who had made a mockery of his imperial majesty's command and was unworthy to come into his presence. Just so, it is a great reproach and dishonor to God if we, to whom he offers and pledges so many inexpressible blessings, despise them or lack confidence that we shall receive them and scarcely venture to ask for a morsel of bread.[8]

Let it be noted: the Reformer points to the fact that the real reason for our renunciation of petitionary prayer might well be our lack of faith—and how much worse it would be if that lack of faith were to be justified theologically!

The true pinnacle of petitionary prayer is the prayer of intercession—prayer for others. Attentive Bible readers will notice that in Christ's parable of the persistent friend, the requester who pesters his friend in the middle of the night does so not for himself but for the needs of someone else he wants to provide for and look after, a third person who has come in hungry late that day. The incident of Christ healing the centurion's man tells the same story about prayer for others. It is therefore above all the prayer of intercession that Jesus encouraged in his disciples.

This task of prayer for others is an essential element of Christian living, and an inexhaustible theme in itself. We could make the petitions of the Lord's Prayer, for example, the theme of intercessory prayer. The Reformers exhorted believers to pray daily for preachers, magistrates, neighbors, one's own house and family, and for the future sustenance of all these.[9] Today we would add a topic they mentioned only occasionally, as a prime concern of prayer for others: the spreading of God's Kingdom through the proclamation of the Gospel. We have said that the prayer of intercession is the weightiest weapon of the "Church militant here on earth." And it is the indispensable presupposition of the two major tasks arising from the Gospel: service and proclamation.

Looking at our own time, we hardly lack reason or urgency for interceding in prayer. Globally, we seem to face one dangerous crisis after another; each one is capable of developing into confrontation and war. Socially, alienation between different opinion groups is mounting to such a degree that we might wonder whether there is any common ground left in these areas.

Paul's testimony tells us that it is the nature of this world to suffer constant corruption, to be pulverized by human wickedness (Ephesians 4:22). Through our prayers of intercession, we add to the forces that sustain the world. "Two pillars support the world, although it attacks them unceasingly: God's providence and command, and the Christians' prayer."[10]

This undergirding nature of prayer raises the question, Do not Christians pray far too seldom for those in government, although they are expressly instructed to do so by the Apostles? Perhaps we too easily overlook what Paul tells us in 1 Timothy 2:1-2—"First of all, then, I urge that supplications, prayers, intercessions, and thanksgivings be made for all men, for kings and all who are in high positions. . . ." Believers would find it easier to understand their responsibility for the life of the nation as well as for the course of events in the Church if they began to exercise that responsibility through intercessory prayer.

The range of our prayer for others includes those closest to us as well as those on the other side of the world from us. But what of its depth? This dimension of our prayer for others is visible in Paul's own great example of prayer for his churches, which can be found in Colossians 1:9-12—

> We have not ceased to pray for you, asking
> that you may be filled with the knowledge of
> his will in all spiritual wisdom and
> understanding . . . to lead a life worthy of the
> Lord [compare Philippians 1:27!], fully pleasing
> to him, bearing fruit in every good work and
> increasing in the knowledge of God . . . strengthened
> with all power, according to his glorious might,
> for all endurance and patience with joy, giving
> thanks to the Father, who has qualified us to
> share in the inheritance of the saints in light.

In comparison with Paul's prayer, our intercession for the individuals God has entrusted to us may still be rather insufficient. But Scripture's promise of answered prayer must be understood with these concrete horizons for nation, missions, and Church: "The prayer of a righteous man [that is, of one who has first prayed for his own purification; the prayer of one who has been forgiven] is powerful and effective" (James 5:16, NIV).

The persistence of prayer

Our final emphasis is that prayer and intercession are to be exercised not just now and then, but consistently and ceaselessly. Martin Luther explains this life of prayer in a vivid picture:

> Therefore, where there is a Christian, there is really the Holy Spirit who does nothing but pray evermore. For even if he does not move his lips or utter words, nevertheless his heart beats and goes incessantly with such sighs: "Oh, dear Father, may it come about that your name be hallowed, your kingdom come, your will be done!" And the more and harder he is pressed and driven by blows and affliction and need, the more and stronger go those sighs and prayers, and orally, too, so that one cannot find a Christian who is without prayer, just as there is no living man without a pulse, which never stops, but beats and stirs always by itself, although that man sleeps or does something else so as not to be aware of it.[11]

This picture of almost unconscious prayer is beautifully drawn. But we must not let it obscure the other side of the truth (which Luther earlier emphasized) that we are also positively urged and commanded to pray actively—because we might forget or cease to do so. Prayer is the beginning of obedience. Jesus dedicated the other parable on prayer, that of the judge pestered by the requests of the persistent widow, to teach that people always ought to pray and not to lose heart. It is just this same attitude that Jesus recommends to his followers, promising, "And will not God vindicate his elect, who cry to him day and night? Will he delay long over them? I tell you, he will vindicate them speedily" (Luke 18:7). Our prayers are to be sustained and tenacious.

But where do we stand in our actual practice of prayer? How consistent and sustained is our personal, individual pursuit of speaking to God and hearing him speak? There's a story that tells of a businessman's ironic remark to his taxi driver, "I'm in a great hurry, so please drive slowly." His business was so important that he wanted to make sure he arrived safely, with nothing more unpleasant befalling him than being a little late to his destination. Someone has pointed out that this should be our attitude in regard to our devotional life: "Today I will be particularly busy; therefore, I need an extended time of prayer this morning."

Wherever we find ourselves losing ground in our prayer life, we must fight back to recover our regular times of quiet, times of meditation on Scripture and in prayer, times of confidential conversation with the Lord every day. Isaiah gently suggests that the early morning is best for these times; Jesus confirms it.

In order to begin our day with sufficient quiet time, however, we will need to exercise all the discipline we can muster to bring the previous day to an end at the right time. There are certainly legitimate problems here: many church activities take place in the evening, for example, and some tend to draw themselves out past 10:00 p.m., necessarily or not. Some of us have trouble falling asleep after such busy evenings. Others battle health problems, especially in unforgiving climates, that make it nearly impossible to rise at an early hour.

Whatever time of day turns out to be best, we must make sure that we have sufficient time alone with God, undisturbed, every day. Without this crucial time, we'll find ourselves soon unable to hold up in other important activities at the right level of quality.

Prayer is *absolutely indispensable*. As Paul says, we must not tire of telling each other the same things again and again (cf. Philippians 3:1). Indeed, there are some truths in Christianity that I need to be reminded of every six hours, because of the short memory of human nature for things spiritual. Among them are prayer, intercession, and the need for an ear attuned to God.

Overall, we must look at prayer as our *privilege*. Our adoption to the status of children of the Heavenly Father comes before our commission to work. Jesus indicates this priority when he says, "No longer do I call you servants. . . . I have called you friends . ." (John 15:15). As Christians, we can be certain of the friendship of Jesus. Then let us also, above and before everything else, practice that friendship in prayer. "Behold, I stand at the door and knock; if anyone hears my voice and opens the door, I will come in to him and eat with him, and he with me" (Revelation 3:20).

Notes

1. Saint Bernard of Clairvaux, *De modo bene vivendi* ("On How to Live Well"), ch. XLIX, 117.
2. John Calvin, *Institutes of the Christian Religion*, III, 20, 9.
3. E. Jünger, *Strahlungen III*, Munich (dtv) 1966, 14.
4. A. Herrlinger, *Die Theologie Melanchthons in ihrer geschichtlichen Entwicklung*, Gotha 1979, 240.
5. Martin Luther, *Large Catechism*, in Th. Tappert, loc. cit., 420.
6. Luther, WA, 10, I, 2, 184, 31 ff. ("Advent Postil," 1522).
7. Luther, *Large Catechism*, loc. cit., 423.
8. Luther, *Large Catechism*, 427 f.
9. Luther, *Large Catechism*, 424.
10. Luther, WA, 45, 535, 5 f. ("On the 14. and 15. Chapter of St. John," 1537).
11. Luther, WA, 541, 31 ff.

5

SUSTAINMENT AND PRESERVATION

Second among the assignments and tasks that are entrusted to a life by the Gospel is sustainment and preservation. This task concerns the work of God in preserving his creation so that it does not fall prey to the forces of destruction. To this divine work we are in constant debt for our provisions and our creational existence.

God's "cultural mandate" calls man to participate in some way in his work of preservation. This commission is made up of the charge to administer God's creation, to "subdue the earth and have dominion over the fish of the sea and over the birds of the air and over every living thing that moves upon the earth" (Genesis 1:28), as well as to "till and keep" (Genesis 2:15) the trust property. The task is stewardship: a dialectic or combination of rule and service (this term occurs in the Hebrew text where the RSV translates "to till"), to the end of preservation. That is God's assignment for man.

Surprisingly, the same concern comes up in the New Testament, addressing the Christian, highlighting the sustainment especially of people. According to Christ's expressed will, his disciples are to take part in the divine work of sustenance and preservation. More than once, Christ describes the disciple in his parables as the *steward* or *householder* enlisted by him. In one of those parables, in Matthew 24:45-51, the parallelism to God's own work in sustaining creation as laid out in Psalm 104:27 becomes immediately evident: The master has put the disciple in charge of his household "to give them their food at the proper time" (NIV). If the disciple loves the master he will also love his master's household and do as he is told.

The ethics of sustainment and preservation are thus necessarily part of Christian ethics. This fact must be upheld against those among us who confess to knowing only Christ's Great Commission, Matthew 28:18-20, and neglect God's cultural mandate, Genesis 1:28 and Genesis 2:15. Later we will have to deal with the reverse of this one-sidedness. Here, however, it needs to be established: God's creation and man's commission in it must not be disregarded or disdained. Christians will have to find the proper balance between the two tasks assigned to them—on one hand, in the preservation of creation; on the other, in the realm of salvation.

Natural resources

Man's task of sustaining creation comes into force first in his attitude toward natural resources, foremost toward food. The little remark made by Christ at the end of the story of the feeding of the five thousand, "Let nothing be wasted" (John 6:12, NIV), has far-reaching relevance. It refers, of course, to the leftovers of food at that and any future occasion, and rules out waste and destruction of victuals. Beyond that, it points his disciples in general to a lifestyle of personal moderation, economy, frugality, and a regular reduction of pretension and consumption. In short, it encourages us to preserve and be careful with what we have been given. It is highly reasonable to apply this point generally to the resources in creation which God laid up there for the use of mankind, be it minerals or the fertility of the ground, as well as air and water.

The idea of a "simple lifestyle" was first thematized at the 1974 Congress on World Evangelism in Lausanne, Switzerland. The "Lausanne Covenant" urges Christians to live a simple lifestyle in order to help direct even more resources to further evangelism and social relief.

Recent years have made us acutely aware of the problems arising from man's management of nature's economy with modern means of efficiency. There are indications that only the instruments of human exploitation and acquisition have become more sophisticated: The avid exploitation of humanity's natural environment and the exploitation of man by man for personal enjoyment are age-old impulses.

Willem A. Visser't Hooft, the first General Secretary of the World Council of Churches, characterized the problem of man's relationship with nature correctly by posing the alternatives, "Dionysus or St. Francis?" He contrasted the pagan attitude of Dionysus, the ancient Greek deity who represented the lifestyle of intoxication, making nature subservient to the end of man's self-enjoyment, to St. Francis' orientation of appreciation for animals and elements as co-creatures of man, which is the truly Christian attitude.[1]

So Christ's exhortation—"Let nothing be wasted"—applies to everybody, the hedonist as well as the indifferent, but also to the unconcerned believer who feels he has no charge regarding his interaction with creation but lives already within the sphere of a future world.

Civil vocation

Next to natural resources, our duties on the basic level of our creaturely existence cluster around a civil vocation. God's creation is clean and good, and so are the callings that serve its preservation.

This affirmation was the point especially made by the Protestant Reformation, in counter-action against the medieval denunciation of "worldly" vocations. The preceding centuries had emphasized the so-called religious vocations of monk, nun, and priest. Against these prevailing values,

Protestantism held that we can also hallow God's name and serve him in our civil vocation, through the sanctification of the workday. Man was to implement God's will in vocation so that, as Martin Luther described it, "a simple and rough-cut tradesman, cobbler or blacksmith, would sit at home, and even if he were dirty and sooty and smelled badly of wax and pitch, would think: my God has made me a husband and given me a house, wife, and children, and ordered me to love them and feed them with the work of my hands."[2] According to the view of the Reformation, the primary duties of vocation and family were supplemented by the duties each one had in civil society.

Most of us are aware of the extent to which liberal theology in the nineteenth century and the social gospel movement in the twentieth century identified with this Reformational stance and praised the individual's work in his creational milieu and civil vocation. Some, like Albrecht Ritschl, the grandfather of modern liberal theology, put particularly strong emphasis on the little phrase "at home" in Luther's description. Ritschl turned this aspect polemically against the general sentiment in the church of his day, which had only just discovered in full the transcultural missionary task.[3] No doubt Luther, Calvin, and the Reformational stance with its motto "Vocational work is worship of God" was at the root of Ritschl's objection.

In the next chapter we will have to voice some criticism of the Protestant piety of vocation and its seemingly unlimited glorification. At this point, however, we need to highlight the positive evaluation of human work, and for our part recognize and respect the task of the Christian in his or her civil vocation—the preservation of creation.

There is a hierarchy of vocations in the Christian life, and this is its foundational level. Chapter six explores the Christian's calling to witness and proclamation; the basic commission, however, needs to be acknowledged first. Nobody must be allowed to revert quickly to allegedly higher or more spiritual activities and then look down his nose at those who stay behind and try to help keep human life going.

Clearly, this is a delicate theme to pursue, especially in consideration of those whose vocation is to work full-time for the Church and missions. In some respects, today's missionaries are the inheritors of the monks of the Middle Ages, because many of these monks were the missionaries and itinerant evangelists of their time. A Bible study on missionary lifestyle would perhaps inevitably lead to that great passage in Matthew 19 that speaks of leaving behind jobs, families, possessions, geographical stability and the security that goes with it, all for the sake of the Kingdom of God. This passage was also the central point of reference for the medieval monks.

The proper establishment of an ethic of missionary existence cannot, however, belittle the tasks and vocations that help sustain human life.

We must not fall into the trap, as some did in the Middle Ages, of singling out the one who has left behind family and civil vocation for the sake of the Gospel as the only true and really serious Christian. If we were to think this way, we would naturally have no message for the lives of the people we evangelize, or even for those who support missionaries financially. And neither would we have any Christian understanding of, for example, the work of homemakers, some of whom, after all, quite directly keep missionaries going. Every Christian is indeed called to witness, but the apostolate, or traveling missionary, is an extraordinary vocation.

We must acknowledge and remember that there are different gifts and ministries in the Body of Christ, and each different member and function is honorable and necessary.

The family
A third essential area of nursing and sustaining is our maintenance and support of the family. The family is God's primary arrangement for the sustenance of creation—a precious gift, if only we would grasp it. We must exert ourselves constantly for this institution, which is a blessing too often uncounted and too easily overlooked.

This affirmation of the family is especially needed in a time such as ours, torn to pieces humanly and socially by destructive forces and circumstances. Christian families can be refuges of protection, islands of human and social recovery and rehabilitation, by safeguarding their own members and sheltering and sustaining others. The frightening statistics on the progressive disintegration of the family in North America, and the consequent social problems of incalculable magnitude that overtax both budgets and welfare agencies, show clearly that safeguarding the family is not a matter of sustaining romantic ideals. Rather, it is of crucial concern in preserving fundamental values of community and life.

Caring for people

In this task of providing and sustaining, the Bible points beyond nature, vocation, and family to a fourth arena—the lives of other people around us, entrusted in some measure to our safekeeping. To each one of us, God commends our neighbor's needs of basic preservation. And the Bible is not at all ethereal about this commission of care; in its view, the good is whatever is "profitable to men" (Titus 3:8).

With this area of nurture we enter the vast field of love of neighbor, the second part of Christ's double commandment of love. We are to be shepherds to people by sustaining them—in the sense of both upholding them and holding them up to God.

Christ's own interest underlying the attention he gave to preserving material resources ("Let nothing be wasted") was the sustainment of people. This concern motivated his feeding of the multitude:

"I am unwilling to send them away hungry, lest they faint on the way" (Matthew 15:22). Evidently, Christian charity must aim at upholding people in all situations of need.

Jesus taught this principle in many instances. The most striking one is his parable of the Good Samaritan, which Jesus told in response to a request for an interpretation of the double commandment of love. He couched his interpretation in a story about an individual act of sustaining a human life in danger. When we study this parable we should not, therefore, rush to spiritualize it as only a picture of what Christ does for us in bringing salvation. Nor should we criticize it by suggesting that he should rather have campaigned for a social change in that country that would make the road to Jericho a safe route for travelers. We dare not dismiss what the parable presents: an immediate, individual act of material support—a concept so easily dismissed by political ideologies.

There is no getting away in the New Testament from the emphasis on personal works of mercy and charity. For Christians, good deeds mean "help [in] cases of urgent need" (Titus 3:14). In this respect, we cannot overlook the seemingly ubiquitous exhortation in the first three gospels to "give to the poor." This connection is confirmed by the equation Jesus makes in Mark 3:4—to do good is to save and sustain life. Matthew 25:31-46, the passage on the six bodily works of mercy, speaks the same language.

The apostle Paul keeps this horizon squarely in view. There is much to learn from a detailed study of chapters 8 and 9 of 2 Corinthians, on the collection taken for the poor churches in Judaea who had met with a period of famine. Paul was convinced that God would give to believers in Corinth above what they needed, so they in turn could give to others. Through a network of churches, the exchange over distance could fulfill God's intention for mutual support and create "equality" (2 Corinthians 8:14).

Today's equivalent of the poor churches in Judaea is perhaps the Ethiopian refugees in neighboring countries, the orphaned children of Uganda, those stricken by drought or floods in Asia, Africa, Latin America. We are surrounded by catastrophic need. Missionaries in severely afflicted countries must make the rich churches across the ocean aware of the plight of their brethren and instruct them in how to help alleviate such suffering.

Another aspect of this task of sustainment is finding work for people. Unemployment will probably be with us for some time to come. Work not only opens the doors to material self-sufficiency and independence, but also to an enhanced sense of personal responsibility and dignity.

We need not look only to disadvantaged countries to discover great human need, however. Lost in comparably well-off countries are the uprooted, the displaced, the disadvantaged and neglected, the suppressed and defenseless, whom the Christian

Church should take in. Not the least of these are the unborn, whose lives are in great peril. Wherever a church makes it its task to sustain and defend them, it can quickly move into a position that calls forth condemnation—and the ostracizing that goes with it—rather than praise, from the surrounding society.

We need to employ the creativity of our imagination, and the resourcefulness of love, to discover how we can best build up and support others, both materially and spiritually. For our task of sustainment clearly does not end with making material provision. Shepherding people means to help them grow; it demands thoughtfulness about "how to make the other one great," and it implies nothing less than the art of true friendship for others. The offering of friendship communicates universally to others; every human being has a sense of such genuine acts. They are almost always recognized gratefully, and often quickly understood as the deeds of love. And who else is better prepared to share the load that others carry than the Christian, who understands that life need no longer revolve around himself because Christ has taken care of his needs and carried his burdens.

Sustaining relationships

This biblical emphasis upon the individual act of supporting another leads naturally into the fifth, and final, area of preservation. The objects of our sustaining and healing are not only individuals, but also the relationships between them—the inter-connected filaments forming a web that joins people and social groups. These filaments are continually wounded and destroyed; our healing influence on them engenders the reconciliation that they so desperately need.

Our task is not merely to become better people ourselves, but to bring healing into the world. Larger tasks wait upon us than the furtherance of our own perfection. We are called to help bring about reconciliation—to bring alienation and divisions between people under the healing sun of the Gospel, so that new life might arise through Christ.

Sustaining and healing human relationships bears fruit in many ways, but one of the most prominent is the extension of others of the forgiveness we ourselves have received from God. To pass on that experience is of enormous importance in the eyes of our Lord. When he gave his disciples what we now call "The Lord's Prayer," he made it a point afterwards to comment on one line in it—the petition, "Forgive us our trespasses, as we have forgiven them who trespassed against us." Jesus said concerning this request, "But if you do not forgive men their trespasses, neither will your Father forgive your trespasses" (Matthew 6:15). Therefore, he concluded, "Whenever you stand praying, forgive, if you have anything against any one; so that your Father also who is in heaven may forgive you your trespasses" (Mark 11:25). We cannot obtain God's forgiveness for ourselves if we hold on to our accusations of, and bitterness toward, another person.

The same truth is also the purpose behind Jesus' parable of the unfaithful servant, who, having been forgiven all his debt, was nevertheless unwilling to forgive the minor items owed to him by others. Such a man might well find his own forgiveness and grace from the Lord withdrawn again from him. Christians are called to be peacemakers, in large part through asking for and granting forgiveness, which can renew human relationships.

The Church in action

These acts of helping and preserving—with natural resources, in civil vocation, in the family, in caring for people, and in sustaining relationships—are nothing else than the good works by which believers become the light of the world and sustain their society. Jesus foresees that these good works will even prompt people to praise our Father in heaven as they see and understand these works (because of the "golden rule"); praise of God, therefore, is the final outcome of these good works (Matthew 5:16).

The task of helping and sustaining is a paramount assignment for the individual Christian. For the whole fellowship or congregation, it is more than obvious from the New Testament that charity is a critically important task. Acts 6 records that the Apostles instituted seven deacons because they recognized the need for competent handling of the "daily distribution" of provisions. They solved the problem (discussed at such length today) of the balance of proclaiming and sustaining by affirming that both are needed.

A parallel example of this dual emphasis is Christ's double commandment of love, which tells us that loving God is the first of two equally valid commandments. We need both proclamation and service. Proclamation is principal, however, because if we do not accept the proclamation of the Gospel, we have no motivation to serve.

Those who work in callings of serving and sustaining, which are often characterized by somewhat repetitious activity, have a professional problem: the Martha syndrome. This problem crops up when individuals become overburdened by the number and sometimes dull nature of their daily chores. To remedy this situation, and to guard against it, Christians involved in this kind of work especially need to make it a rule to go back and, like Mary, sit at the feet of Jesus and listen—the one essential thing. They also need to rehearse, again and again, the key gifts and tasks of the Gospel—forgiveness, commission, counsel, prayer.

Those whose ministry is with the Word of God have this same need. They must make sure they take time for prayer, for worship, and for personal Bible study—times of feeding on God's Word and recovering the freshness of the Christian faith.

Without such times of personal renewal in the Lord, the character of witness in Christian ministry will suffer.

A Christian church is not complete, in New Testament terms, without a strong program of charitable work—looking after the needy, the sick and disabled, and those in prison. In this respect, Scripture's exhortations first address those Christians who in today's world live in well-protected circumstances. These men and women are to become the Good Samaritans, or the shepherds and benefactors, toward those in need.

The proper organization of a congregation today would address this ministry of shepherding the needy by reinstituting, where necessary, the ministry of deacon next to those of pastor-teacher and missionary. It was through a division of work that the Apostles made certain that neither prayer and proclamation nor charity was neglected. Although in their individual lives Christians certainly have all these assignments of prayer, charity, and witness, in the context of their contribution churchwide they have different functions. And we need them all.

Notes

1. *Foi et Vie* 73 (1974), Nos. 5-6, 176 ff.
2. Martin Luther, WA, 32, 325, 36 ff. ("Exposition of the Sermon on the Mount," 1532).
3. A. Ritschl, *Christian Perfection*, Bibliotheca Sacra 35 (1878), 656-680.

6

PROCLAMATION

The Gospel does not reach its final goal in ourselves. Our Lord indicated this truth when, in promising the Holy Spirit, he declared, "But the water that I shall give him [he who comes to believe in Jesus] will become in him a well of water springing up into everlasting life" (John 4:14). This is the appropriate image for the life of the disciple of Christ, who not only receives the Gospel but is also empowered to pass it on.

The third predominant task of a life lived by the Gospel involves the proclamation of the Gospel, or the spiritual sustainment and furtherance of people. In the wider sense of the Great Commission, it is the "life-changing" task of missions.

God enables us to share the Gospel. But this ministry is also a consequence of gratitude for salvation received. Christ's rule that "out of the abundance of the heart the mouth speaks" (Matthew 12:34) is valid not just negatively, but also positively. This is Paul's logic, too, as in his assertion in 2 Corinthians 4:13 that "we too believe, and so we speak," and in his statement in Romans 10:10, "With the heart one believes to righteousness, and with the mouth confession is made to salvation."

Faith steps outside of itself into the world in self-expression, by declaring Christ before people. Notice the same linkage between gratitude for salvation received and public witness in the psalmist's impassioned declaration, "What shall I render to the Lord for all his bounty to me? I will lift up the cup of salvation and call on the name of the Lord, I will pay my vows to the Lord in the presence of all his people" (Psalm 117:12). "Faith . . . is firm and active. No faith is firm that does not show itself in confession."[1]

Here the most intimate meets with a global horizon. In this way the prophet prays, "My soul yearns for thee in the night, my spirit within me earnestly seeks thee. For when thy judgments come to the earth, the inhabitants of the world learn righteousness" (Isaiah 26:9). Conversation with God in the stillness of the night or early morning communicates wisdom and insights that often serve the welfare of humanity to an unexpected extent. What we have perceived in quietness before God does not belong to us alone. Perhaps this is the way to understand Christ's somewhat enigmatic saying in Matthew 10:27, "What I tell you in the dark, utter in the light; and what you hear whispered, proclaim upon the housetops." It is also true that times of prayer and study of Scripture unrelated to the horizon of humanity and the outside world lose much of their relevance.

In defense of proclamation

The task of proclamation—the preaching of God's standards and his message of salvation—clearly goes beyond our regular vocational work and the immediate service we render to creation. Here is where we must be critical of some Reformational perspectives. The Reformers' panegyric of vocation sometimes comes across so exclusively that it tempts us to think that in their view of the Gospel, practically considered, Christ intended to make his disciples better fishermen ("at home"!) instead of apostles. At one point even Luther ventured such a theory. In his exposition of John 21 Luther comments, "The Risen One lets his disciples continue their fishing trade at the Sea of Galilee." The point Luther wants to make is, "The Lord does not tear apart through the Gospel what pertains to government and the economy."[2] True enough; however, he does call some in such a manner that they bring their boats ashore and leave both family and trade behind. His calling surpasses, and takes precedence over, civil vocation.

Perhaps we are faced at this point with a blind spot in the Reformers' thinking. Their view of vocation is understandable as a reaction against medieval monastic theology, with its devaluation of civil life. But their reaction did cost Protestantism two hundred years of foreign missions. Only early Pietism, with its resolute regression to Scripture, became aware of this case of distorted vision and rectified the situation.

Luther at least made the propagation of the Gospel throughout the world a topic of intercession, in his exposition of the second petition of the Lord's Prayer in his *Large Catechism*:

> We pray here at the outset that all this [i.e., the Kingdom of God] may be realized in us and that God's name may be praised through his holy Word and our Christian lives. This we ask, both in order that we who have accepted it may remain faithful and grow daily in it, and in order that it may gain recognition and followers among other people and advance with power throughout the world . . . so that many may come into the kingdom of grace and become partakers of salvation. . . .

And again a little later: "Dear Father, we pray thee, give us first of all thy Word, that the Gospel may be sincerely preached throughout the world, and," in addition, "that it may be received by faith and may work and live in us . . . so that thy kingdom may prevail among us through the Word and the power of the Holy Spirit, that the devil's kingdom may be overthrown. . . ."[3]

This request is surely well spoken, and we would indeed make considerable spiritual progress if we prayed like this every day. We can also be especially grateful to Luther for the profundity with which these lines address the question of the present state of God's Kingdom and its advance with us and in us, because it is doubtful whether we are willing to accept this point of view and think in these terms.

On the other hand, we cannot overlook Luther's articulation of this vision in somewhat reduced terms. The progress of the Kingdom is largely limited to the realm "in us"—that is, in those "who have accepted it." The obvious next question raised here is, Through whom is the advance of the Kingdom *in the world* to be implemented? The question that Luther neither asks nor answers is, Who is to take the Gospel to the four corners of the earth? That question would be appropriate, by reference to the Great Commission.

The situation is not much different with another Reformer, Philip Melanchthon. Melanchthon does raise his eyes to the wider horizon of a life devoted to the concerns of the Kingdom of Christ, in at least one passage. In his *Apology for the Augsburg Confession* he addresses the motivations and the contents of Christian good works (and so the practical aspects of "living by the Gospel") and calls good works the means with which Christ demonstrates his rule to the outside world: "The dangers, labors, and sermons of the apostle Paul, Athanasius, Augustine, and other teachers of the church are holy works." These, as well as suffering for Christ's sake, but also every deed of Christian charity (e.g., Paul's collection for the church at Jerusalem), the mortification of the flesh, and Christian discipline, are real battles by which Christ restrains the devil and drives him away. To disparage these works "would be to disparage the outward administration of Christ's rule among men."[4]

That seems to be as far as Melanchthon goes in this direction, however. His text contains the references to exactly those perspectives that govern the third task of a life lived by the Gospel: proclamation. But these references seem to constitute an isolated stance within the body of Reformational writings in several respects. It almost sounds like the *Apology* granting to its confessional adversary, the theologians of the Roman Church, a point that is obviously supported by Scripture and church history. Already the unusual concept of "the outward administration of Christ's rule among men" witnesses to that.

And the context of Melanchthon's remarks corroborate this sense of an isolated stance. For Melanchthon immediately returns to the praise of those good works that the Christian is to do in his private life and civil vocation. Correspondingly, he treats the reader once more to the story, so much loved by the Reformers, of that cobbler in the city of Alexandria whom God had shown to St. Anthony, the father of Christian monasticism, as truly living in the state of perfection. A cobbler? When Antonius interviewed the man, he replied only that he did nothing special. In the morning he prayed for the city, and then he went about his trade.[5]

According to the Reformers, that way of living was perfection. They used this story from the early Church frequently in order to inculcate their new ideal of a life of divine worship within one's civil vocation. And indeed, the Alexandrian cobbler lived with a perspective larger than what we usually take into consideration: he prayed for "the city." He simply obeyed the biblical exhortation in Jeremiah 29:7—"Seek the welfare of the city where I have sent you into exile, and pray to the Lord on its behalf."

This same perspective and obedient response should be expected from Christians in the twentieth century. It would give us a new authority in our conversation with people and for our proclamation of the Gospel. We are commissioned to think responsibly for the welfare of a city or country, and to exercise this responsibility first in our prayer of intercession. We ought to concern ourselves *daily* with the state of the Kingdom of God in our own neighborhood, beginning with the acknowledgment of God's commandments and including the question of the reception of the Gospel. If necessary, we need to ask God to widen our thinking in this respect.

All of this needs to be said in support of the Alexandrian cobbler. In the context of Melanchthon's Apology, however, the stress is of course laid on the other specification made in the cobbler's response to St. Anthony: In the view of the

Reformation, perfection consists in the good man going about his trade ("at home") instead of giving himself to monastic vagabondism and the like! Christian perfection was to be found "on the spot," in one's everyday work in a civil vocation.

It is precisely at this point where we must go beyond the creational concerns of the Reformers—civil vocation and the sustainment of life—and emphasize the other side, in order to recover the wider horizon of the Kingdom of God as it "advances with power throughout the world." Contrary to much Reformational and Protestant teaching, the Kingdom of God is not limited to honest work in one's civil vocation, and in providing for one's family. Certainly we must honor the cobbler of Alexandria; but that cannot mean that we close our eyes to the challenge of another cobbler, William Carey, who left his trade behind and went out to Calcutta to become an apostle to India. We must become students of spiritual geopolitics.

We are reminded of this wider horizon by, among other things, the list of priorities given us in the order of the petitions of the Lord's Prayer. There, the first three petitions are concerned with the honor of God's name, the coming of the Kingdom of God, and the implementation of God's will. Only then, with the fourth petition, do we pray for the material means of subsistence for which we labor in our vocations. Jesus said, "Seek first his kingdom . . . and all these things shall be yours as well" (Matthew 6:33). As the context of this passage shows, we would be assuming a pagan attitude if we reversed the order of petition and concern.

This sequence must also be observed again by Protestant ethics when it sets out to describe life by the Gospel. Protestant ethics cannot (as has so often happened until now) come to a halt with the praise of work in civil vocation and exclude the Great Commission as a kind of irregularity in the Christian life—which is handled as an appendix to practical theology and as a perpetual oddity, to be studied only by a few so inclined. Especially today, when we have begun to comprehend seriously that God has indeed entrusted believers with the care of the material well-being of their fellow-men in the world, we need to keep the list of priorities given in the Lord's Prayer constantly in mind.

The reawakening of a Christian passion for just social conditions is a good thing—and in some quarters it is long overdue. But we must think beyond it and ask ourselves, Do we still have a message for those who have been successfully provided with the means of material subsistence? Or we need to ask, Have we fully reached our goals when jobs, homes, and provisions have been procured—for example, for refugees who settle in our own lands? Is not ours an assignment that goes beyond material concerns, a charge that must come to mind as we encounter, for example, members of other religions (or, indeed, atheists) who live in our midst? It is here that we must remember our obligation to proclaim the Gospel, an obligation that we may already be in the process of forgetting.

We dearly need to lend our ear to another exhortation of Martin Luther's, which looks back at the question of priorities:

> It is now my sincere counsel and warning that you be careful and insist on this sole question of what makes a person a Christian, and let by no means some other question or concern be equal to it. If someone suggests something new, you must begin asking him: "Dear man, would this also make a Christian or not?" If not, don't let it become the cardinal question.[6]

Is not the same need true today? Right in our midst, and especially in a society quickly becoming secular, there are so many places where the Gospel is not known and still has to be made known. Many people, in fact, have not ever heard it. How can we think of teaching them the ethics of the Gospel, "to do good and share" (Hebrews 13:16), if we haven't taught them the Gospel beforehand?

"What makes a person a Christian?" Perhaps in this question we encounter today a task that especially addresses the evangelicals among us who have always identified with this choice of priority. They should make it their task to raise general Christian consciousness of this need.

That kind of task invites singlemindedness and tenacity. For the apostle Paul, what counted in any given situation was the furtherance, the defense, and the confirmation of the Gospel (see Philippians 1:7, 12). Christians at the end of the twentieth century must recapture Paul's charge to Timothy, "Preach the word . . . in season and out of season" (2 Timothy 4:2). Proclamation takes a measure of tenacity: "I have not restrained my lips, as thou knowest, O Lord" (Psalm 40:9). A bit more passion for God's name to be hallowed in our time, a little more passion for the furtherance of his concerns, would be quite becoming. In church and theology, one ought to be able to sense whether someone is committed to that pursuit. Christians of all persuasions, living in a society still widely characterized by affluence, should renounce the notorious dedication to their much-loved private lives. Rather than holding to their compromise of piety and the pleasures of life, they should stand up and be counted, they should let themselves be heard in the land, and they should seek God's Kingdom right there through prayer and proclamation, word and deed.

Not a few Christians have long become used to identifying with the so-called "silent majority," or "those who are quiet in the land" (Psalm 35:20). It would be quite improper, however, to use that verse as a justification of one's silence in the public place. Once we read the phrase of "those who are quiet in the land" in its context, we can easily see what it does and doesn't mean: "to be quiet" means to relinquish taking one's rights into one's own hands. But at the same time those "quiet" people pray for their adversaries, they give thanks to God "in the great congregation, in the mighty throng" they praise him and speak of his deeds of righteousness (Psalm 35:18, 28). How else can we reconcile the concept of "those who are quiet in the land" with the New Testament testimony of "we too believe, and so we speak" (2 Corinthians 4:13), and with the expectation that others will see their good works and glorify their Father who is in heaven (Matthew 5:16)? These passages should be understood as necessary correctives by those who hesitate to go and speak out and serve through word and deed, lest they fail to fulfill their commission and their destiny as light in the world.

We can see, then, that proclamation is necessary both from the nature of faith and the need of the world, and that its rank and relevance among Christian activities is primary. What are some of the distinctive forms that proclamation takes?

Evangelism and teaching

Within the overall concept of proclamation, we must always make the basic distinction between evangelism (or initial proclamation) and teaching. It has been observed in the gospels that after his public messages Jesus withdrew with the small group of his disciples into a retreat, in order to teach them in more depth. This coupled approach has also been termed the *extensive* and *intensive* aspects of proclamation.

Paul acknowledged this two-pronged approach. "I have planted, Apollos watered, but God gave the growth," he declared (1 Corinthians 3:6). At some points, he himself returned to the places he had evangelized in order to "strengthen the souls of the disciples" (Acts 14:22, cf. 15:32), or he traveled the same itinerary a second time "to strengthen all the disciples" (Acts 18:23). Moreover, he spent at least two-and-a-half years in Ephesus and stayed quite some time in Corinth, facts that are easily concealed by our general reference to the "journeys of Paul."

We must not turn the idea that Paul was ever pressing on to new places into a missionary speed method of our own—where we sweep through places with an evangelistic campaign and exact no energy in working to give roots to faith. For Paul, the context or starting point was more often than not with groups of proselytes and devout (Acts 13:43, for example), former heathen who gathered around the synagogues and no doubt already had substantial knowledge of the basic teachings of the Old Testament Scriptures and training in how to run a fellowship. The early Christian worship services were not much different in structure from the synagogue services, and the same parallelism may also apply to much of the structuring of the congregation itself. Paul could assume many of those things. If we go as missionaries today into unevangelized fields we cannot presuppose that knowledge, and consequently will have to take much more time to give root to the young tree we may have planted by the grace of God. There will have to be pre-evangelism, and much more post-evangelism.

We hear news today that backsliding among new Christians and even the extinction of some new churches in Asia are due to a lack of teaching. Those congregations are still volatile, and susceptible to the changing winds of doctrine and human opinion. Today's converts from paganism—as well as those from secular Western society—have to be given a whole new framework of thought and life to be at home in. This need makes obvious demands on the manner, depth, and quality of preaching.

In this respect, the currently popular philosophy of "church planting" could turn out to be dangerously deficient in its concealment of the question of whose responsibility it is to "water" the new plantation. This unguarded talk of "church planting" tends to perpetuate the type of touch-and-go mission that does not follow up evangelism with intensive teaching and faith with love. In contrast to this imbalanced process, Paul took it upon himself to "strengthen the brethren" regularly, and, as we can see from his letters to Timothy and Titus, assumed the overall responsibility not only for the establishment, but also for the spiritual consolidation and advance, of the new churches.

We should all be agreed that a constant repetition of the primary evangelistic message is not sufficient to educate a church. New believers must be led deeper into Scripture to become "dyed in the wool" Christians, in terms of a biblical view of life and world. This naturally entails giving a strong emphasis and endowment to theological seminaries and Bible schools, as well as to local extension courses. Teaching also includes Christian education, so that "One generation shall laud thy works to another, and shall declare thy mighty acts" (Psalm 145:4).

Another pair of categories—and again, not alternatives—refers to the group and the individual and the twin addressees of proclamation and teaching. Evangelism can use mass meetings; teaching is more effective in the small group, as we see in Jesus' strategy. Counseling is the application of both evangelism and teaching to the individual. As it has been said: It's no good trying to heal a person's eye disease by pouring out medication from a second-floor window onto a crowd below. Christianity cannot advance without due concern for the individual person.

Overall, in the formation of a church, it seems wisest to lay full emphasis on training the small group of people who can later carry on the work by themselves.

I will never forget the counsel given to me by a friend from Oxford when I first started work as a student pastor, or university missioner. There were 20,000 students, and I was perplexed by the vastness of my task. My friend wrote,

Here we have completely stopped running large meetings to make the news. Whatever we do, we

invest into the lives of ten or twelve people whom
we know and pray for by name, and hope to give
such a deep experience of the Cross that they can
become pillars of God's work all over the world.
If we feel that it is right for the sake of one of
them to have a large meeting, we'll have one. But
everything we do goes into and is centered around
those individuals.

That counsel brought me welcome relief. In a
time of quiet, I was soon made aware of the names
of five or six people to concentrate on in this
way. I would meet them frequently and address
their personal concerns in many of my given activities. I would even write my annual university
sermon, which had a large audience, just for one
of them. In hindsight, I realize that we actually
ended up with a three-decker principle: the large
meeting, the small group, and individual conversation, all interlocked.

The means of proclamation embraces yet a
third pair of categories—the spoken word and
printed literature. Christians are usually convinced of the pertinence of preaching and proclamation by word-of-mouth. However, many still
need to understand that literature work is the
second leg of Christian proclamation. Surely we
are meant to use the full range of media. But
because many Christians today seem to under-
estimate the relevance of the printed word, it
deserves special attention.

When John Wesley faced for the first time the possibility of open-air preaching in Bristol and was uncertain of whether to proceed, he drew lots. The lot he received read, "Preach and print!" Wesley followed this injunction faithfully indeed for the rest of his life. For the next fifty years, his biographers tell us, he would never let a week pass by without having made something ready for the printer. At the same time, Wesley normally preached two or three times each day of the week.

Today, 250 years later, Christians need to recover Wesley's awareness of the power of this two-pronged approach to proclamation. The printed word is a tool ready for renewed appropriation. Everyone can have a part. A good friend once exhorted me to follow the principle of "Pen and People." Literature needs writers, but it also needs distributors, and most of all readers. It can serve both evangelism and teaching, and it can often reach beyond the range of our spoken word. Let us, therefore, fully activate this field of work and give it our attention, support, and participation every day, from now on.

The goal of proclamation

After these considerations of the range of proclamation with regard to its forms and means, we will conclude with a word on the goal of our proclamation in terms of contents. We have already emphasized a fairly broad understanding of proclamation, as including both teaching and counseling.

On the occasion of his farewell Paul said to the elders of Ephesus, "I did not shrink from declaring to you anything that was profitable. . . . I did not shrink from declaring to you the whole counsel of God" (Acts 20:20, 27).

At this point, we need to remind ourselves that our overall commission is nothing less than to bring people to God—to make disciples, or, as Paul put it, to render every man mature before God in Christ. Thus the goal of all Christian mission—of proclamation, counseling, and teaching—is changing lives; it is helping people come to the point where they truly love God with all their heart and mind, and where they love their neighbor as themselves. For that is also the goal of Christ's work of reconciliation, the restoration of broken covenants. Our struggle, therefore, is for changed men and women to be the result of everything we do.

In a modern art form, the purpose of proclamation has been captured well in the poem "Prayer" by Solzhenitsyn. Looking back on his pilgrimage, he expresses his gratitude that he, too, had been enabled for a while "to mediate to humanity a reflection of your radiance and splendor." Exactly that task is also ours in proclaiming the Gospel.

But even though we may outwardly be professionals of the proclamation of the Word of God, there is really great poverty and superficiality in our performance of that task. Instead of mediating "a reflection of his radiance" we find ourselves producing so much mediocrity, often only a dim and colorless rendering of the message. Far too often, we are like opaque mirrors, or clogged pipes. We seem to suffer from a constant deterioration and narrowing of vision. Sometimes the Church is the worst possible collection of people, its meetings dry as dust, and the last place where one would expect to get a glimpse of God's splendor. Beyond the disappointment of church meetings, however, lies a more fundamental question: How can fallible human beings ever give adequate expression to the grandeur and goodness of God?

At this junction, the subject of proclamation necessarily points back to our very first topic, forgiveness. Forgiveness is a presupposition to proclamation, and most needed by those whose ministry is with God's Word. The story of the calling of Isaiah points out that a cleansing of lips was needed before the prophet could be God's messenger. We need the same cleansing, and we need it day after day. And, indeed, God is able to touch our mouths again and again: "Behold, this has touched your lips; your guilt is taken away and your sin forgiven" (Isaiah 6:7). He himself creates the necessary presupposition for our commission to proclamation, so that we, too, can respond, "Here am I! Send me" (Isaiah 6:8).

Notes
1. Philip Melanchthon, in Th. Tappert, loc. cit., 166.
2. Martin Luther, WA, 32, 67, 1 ff. ("Sermon on Wednesday after Easter," 1530).

3. Luther, in Th. Tappert, loc, cit., 427.
4. Melanchthon, in Th. Tappert, loc. cit., 133.
5. Melanchthon, in Th. Tappert, 275 ff.
6. Luther, WA, 15, 394,1 ff. ("A Letter to the Christians in Strassburg against the Spirit of the Fanatics," 1524).

THE ROOTS
OF RENEWAL

What are the roots of renewal that the Gospel is planting in our world today—in prayer, in teaching, in proclamation, in works of charity? Especially in light of the task of proclamation, two arenas seem to be especially crucial: 1) the larger arena of Christianity's present encounter with secularism— the anti-God or atheistic attitude as a fundamental presupposition of our times and its different phenomena in today's public debates; and 2) a more narrow one of the future developments within Christian theology.

In the larger arena of Christianity's confrontation with the predominating culture, secularism today seems to have quietly assumed power over many areas of life. It seems to have taken authority both in the media and in the world of education, and to be determinative for the future of society.

Questions that engage public discussion are now usually decided in favor of a secular viewpoint. As the public media bear out, the questions of God, his commandments, and his Gospel have become obsolete in practical terms. The idea of Christ's substitutionary atonement for us on the Cross, which is central to the Christian faith, has been lost and abandoned in many places.

The same abandonment of God and his truth is unfortunately true in a number of churches. Even where people still speak of sin and guilt, such discussion is more in the context of a general notion of forgiveness or an assumption of some divine amnesty, rather than on the grounds of Christ's sacrificial passion. Our age is at the point of destroying, first theoretically, and then most certainly also practically, the glory of God in both creation and salvation.

Spearheading this destruction is the atheism of the West. In the final analysis, this atheism is characterized by its incomprehension and rejection of salvation, of the "Lamb of God who takes away the sin of the world" (John 1:29). And sometimes, theologians have every appearance of helping along that failure to comprehend and accept.

We seem to experience today a repetition of the situation of the early Church, which found itself engaged in continuing spiritual confrontation with the intellectual and practical paganism of its time.

In his Doctrine of God, Karl Barth has declared very impressively that it is the task of theology to

"in each and all of its divisions and subdivisions . . .
first and last, as a whole and in part, say nothing
else but God is."[1] On the other hand, it is unfor-
tunate that somewhere else he made comments of
a kind that caused his disciples to drop the traditional Christian task of apologetics—that is, the
defense of the Christian faith—as superfluous and
not worthy of the attention of a Christian theologian. Many have understood those comments to say
that theology no longer owes the world the testimony and assertion that God is—and that he is Lord.

The Christian confrontation with secularism is
not finished, and no segment of Christianity is exempt
from that task. We all need to recover a concentration on the proclamation of God's existence and
kingship with all our statements and declarations.

What is at the root of our lack of Christian
passion and perspective? Everyone seems to pursue
his own theological or ecclesiastical pet idea, and
thus sees only a limited sector of the battle. There
are far too few who think in terms of strategy,
who turn their eyes from the many individual topics
of confrontation to their common source, to the
central theme of our time: man's apostasy, his rebellion against and forgetfulness of God. It isn't good
enough today to think only in terms of the success
or welfare of our particular church or group or
school while the overall situation is rapidly dete-
riorating. And it does not suffice to battle superficially on single issues when the phenomena
deplored are but symptoms of a deeper disease.

The second arena ripe for penetration by the Gospel lies within the territories of Church and theology themselves. Here, uncertainty regarding the object of Christian proclamation is the order of the day in many places, thus making the very task of proclamation doubtful. If there is to be a renewal of the Church, there must also be a renewal of theology, whose task it is to give orientation to the Church, set its direction, and focus its proclamation. Thus theology itself needs to be profoundly refocused to that "light to our path," the Word of God (Psalm 119:105). The life and thought of the Church today must be healed at the source. As Hannah Moore put it, it is no use to pour scent on a stream when its spring is polluted.

Here again, a special challenge to work toward that renewal of theology may be waiting for those who call themselves evangelicals. Evangelicalism in its origins produced some of the ablest theologians of their times. In fact, both in Puritanism and Pietism, evangelicalism began as a program for renewal of Church *and* theology. Today's evangelicals should not rest content with a lesser horizon. They, too, have a responsibility for the course of events in theology and the Church. They must recommit themselves to help Church and theology everywhere hold firmly to God's Word.

Christians of all persuasions need to wake up to an awareness of these ongoing struggles. In the words of G. K. Chesterton, they will make the world beautiful again by beholding it as the battlefield that it is: "When we have defined the evil thing, the colors come back into everything else."[2] Under the perspectives of good and evil, God and secularism, there is more drama in the twentieth century than would ever be necessary to give profile to our lives. Sometimes our days get dull, because we forget the perspective of the battle that is often waged so invisibly and silently. But it is above all in these struggles that we today find the concrete concerns for our prayer, intercession, proclamation, and teaching. It is here that we are called to participate in those "real battles of Christ" spoken of by Melanchthon the Reformer. They are prepared for us and assigned to us by the highest Authority, if we indeed strive to be found living by the Gospel.

Notes
1. Karl Barth, *Church Dogmatics*, Vol. II, 1 (Edinburgh: T. & T. Clark, 1957), 258.
2. As quoted by A. Stone Dale, *The Outline of Sanity: A Life of G. K. Chesterton* (Grand Rapids: Eerdmans, 1982), 48.